Making *The Real World*

Making *The Real World*

a study of a television series

Andrew Hart
and the Southampton Media Education Research Group
with the support of the Television South Community
Unit

The right of the
University of Cambridge
to print and sell
all manner of books
was granted by
Henry VIII in 1534.
The University has printed
and published continuously
since 1584.

CAMBRIDGE UNIVERSITY PRESS
Cambridge
New York   *New Rochelle*
Melbourne   *Sydney*

Published by the Press Syndicate of the University of Cambridge
The Pitt Building, Trumpington Street, Cambridge CB2 1RP
32 East 57th Street, New York, NY 10022, USA
10 Stamford Road, Oakleigh, Melbourne 3166, Australia

First published 1988

Printed in Great Britain at the University Press, Cambridge

British Library cataloguing in publication data

Hart, Andrew
    Making *The Real World*: a study of a television series.
    1. Real World (Television programme)
    I. Title II. Southampton Media Education Research Group
    791.45'72   PN1992.8.D6

    ISBN 0–521–35773–X

Library of Congress cataloguing in publication data

Hart, Andrew.
    1. Real world (Television program)   2. Television programs – Great
    Britain.   3. Television – Production and direction.
    I. Southampton Media Education Research Group.
    II. TVS (Firm: Great Britain).
    Community Unit.   III. Title.
    PN1992.77.R43H37   1988   86–10848
    ISBN 0 521 35773 X

'The Quagga' from *Collected Poems* by D. J. Enright (Oxford
University Press) is reproduced by permission of Watson, Little.
'The Quagga Gets Ready to Gallop Again' from the *Guardian* is
reproduced by permission of Anthony Tucker.

Naming 'the things that are absent' is breaking the spell of things that are.

Nicholas Garnham, *Structures of Television*

To complement *Making The Real World*, and by the same team . . .

TEACHING TELEVISION: THE REAL WORLD

A media education resource, consisting of two elements:

* *A television study resource pack*, which includes a comprehensive range of teaching ideas for use in secondary schools, and further and higher education.

* *The video: a case-study of Dead as the Dodo?* including the complete programme from the TVS series, *The Real World*, interviews with members of the programme team and additional material linked to the teaching ideas.

Details of how to order the resource pack and the video are available from:

Cambridge University Press
(Home Sales Department)
The Edinburgh Building
Shaftesbury Road
Cambridge
CB2 2RU

Teaching Television
The Community Unit
TVS
Southampton
SO9 5HZ
(0703) 834297

The Quagga

By mid-century there were two quaggas left,
And one of the two was male.
The cares of office weighed heavily on him.
When you are the only male of a species,
It is not easy to lead a normal sort of life.

The goats nibbled and belched in casual content;
They charged and skidded up and down their concrete mountain.
One might cut his throat on broken glass,
Another stray too near the tigers.
But they were zealous husbands; and the enclosure was always full,
Its rank air throbbing with ingenuous voices.

The quagga, however, was a man of destiny.
His wife, whom he had met rather late in her life,
Preferred to sleep, or complain of the food and the weather.
For their little garden was less than paradisiac,
With its artificial sun that either scorched or left you cold,
And savants with cameras eternally hanging around,
To perpetuate the only male quagga in the world.

Perhaps that was why he failed to do it himself.
It is all very well for goats and monkeys –
But the last male of a species is subject to peculiar pressures.
If ancient Satan had come slithering in, perhaps . . .
But instead the savants, with cameras and notebooks,
Writing sad stories of the decadence of quaggas.

And then one sultry afternoon he started raising Cain.
This angry young quagga kicked the bars and broke a camera;
He even tried to bite his astonished keeper.
He protested loud and clear against this and that,
Till the other animals became quite embarrassed
For he seemed to be calling them names.

Then he noticed his wife, awake with the noise,
And a curious feeling quivered round his belly.
He was Adam: there was Eve.
Galloping over to her, his head flung back,
He stumbled, and broke a leg, and had to be shot.

D. J. ENRIGHT

Contents

The Southampton Media Education Research Group

Robin Blake   *Cricklade College, Andover, Hants.*
Sue Hackman   *Queen Mary's College, Basingstoke, Hants.*
Alun Hicks   *Ansford School, Somerset.*
Rob Keighley   *Alderman Quilley School, Eastleigh, Hants.*
Hugh Notley   *Corfe Hills School, Corfe Mullen, Dorset.*
Alec Roberts   *Bohunt School, Liphook, Hants.*

The above are all practising teachers in secondary or tertiary education. They are also former students on the MA (Ed.) in Language, Literature and Media Studies at the University of Southampton.

Hilary Durman is Education Officer for TVS and was formerly Head of Drama at Tynemouth College.

Neil Ryder is Senior Lecturer in the Centre for Educational Studies at King's College, London and author of *Science, Television and the Adolescent.*

Andrew Hart is Lecturer in the Department of Education at Southampton University where he teaches postgraduate courses in media studies. He is editor of *Media-in-Education Research* and has produced several media packages for teachers. He has a particular interest in children and television and has written extensively about media in education.

Acknowledgements

This book is the result of contributions from a number of people with similar interests in media education. Our Research Group was formed from teachers who had all studied television as postgraduates. Working with them during the project has been a great privilege and pleasure. Robin Blake, Sue Hackman, Alun Hicks, Rob Keighley, Hugh Notley and Alec Roberts all gave generously of their time and expertise and made substantial original contributions (chapters 2, 3, 5 and 6).

Our debt to the pioneering work of Len Masterman, Neil Ryder and Roger Silverstone should be self-evident, but deserves a special mention here. We have not tried primarily to develop new theories or critical approaches but to draw on existing work and make it accessible.

We should also like to thank the much wider constituency of teachers and advisers who helped us. Their ideas and comments have been most constructive: we hope that users of the package will reap the benefit of this formative process. We are particularly grateful for the advice of the BFI's Education Department, of members of the Southampton Media Education Group and of Julian Bowker who was on secondment at TVS during the project.

Our biggest debt of gratitude, however, must go to TVS who not only funded the research but gave us unprecedented access to the workings of *The Real World*. We should especially like to thank Hugh Geach and Hilary Durman. Hilary not only contributed to the teaching ideas, to the video interviews and to chapter 4 of the book, but she also met our exacting demands with energetic commitment. Our work called on the time and efforts of the already over-stretched staff and resources of the TVS Community Unit. In this respect, we

x   Acknowledgements

should also like to thank Sarah Naughton and Hazel Gale for all their patient hard work and support.

Many other TVS staff made indispensable contributions from an early stage, particularly members of *The Real World* team. We are especially grateful to Greg Dyke, previously Director of Programmes, Mike Southgate, Controller of Programme Organisation and Finance, Peter Williams, Controller of Factual Programmes, and John Huins, then Public Relations Manager, for their help and co-operation; to Mike Mitchell, Karen Avison, Bob Franklin, Mike Hunt and Sue Massey; and especially to Garfield Kennedy, Michael Rodd and Thelma Rumsey, who gave generously of their time and agreed to be interviewed on video.

Finally I should like to express my personal thanks to Jean Hart for her advice, support and resilience; and to Keith Rose and Martin Moore at Cambridge University Press for their patience and enthusiasm.

Andrew Hart
January 1988

Preface

The choice
Common sense science
Television and science

How can we best understand the complex conversation between television producers and their viewers? The difficulty is one of contentious issues made inaccessible by nebulous concepts. Yet there are important problems of power, knowledge and culture to grapple with if we are to understand a set of institutions which are central to our society. This book aims to make some of these concepts concrete, to unravel the threads of these contentious issues and to show how these institutions actually work.

It does so by focusing on a single programme and looking at it within its context. The programme is unpacked gradually like a set of Chinese boxes. Layer by layer its use of television technology, its structure, its use of expert contributors and its relation to sister programmes in a series is revealed. A clear view emerges of the company that made it, the Independent Television system in which that company vies for survival and for greater power, and finally of the audiences who derive pleasure from it and try to make sense of it.

The choice

Before we look at *The Real World*, we need to consider the way science and television engage with everyday life. What is at stake? Everyday life throws up an enormous variety of practical and imaginative problems: can science help to solve any of these? Equally, the world of science throws up problems too: what role does understanding these play in our everyday lives? Above all, does television contribute to our understanding? Could it even undermine this understanding?

What is at stake is a question about a particular kind of power, about autonomy in personal and social life. It turns on whether individuals are empowered to participate in debates about the issues that concern or excite them, or whether they should depend largely on experts. Where is the line drawn in the individual's best interests?

The model of science a producer uses will largely determine the kind of contribution he makes to this process of empowering. It turns out that television science consistently puts forward a preferred model of scientific progress – a model which assumes the need for simplification and resolution of scientific issues for a popular audience. Is this closed model the only one with which the popular audience can operate? Or is there an alternative 'common sense' science model which would be better?

Common sense science

Modern philosophy of science describes something much more open than the media model. It is worth asking whether an open, science-like way of thinking could be constructed out of the elements of common sense.

In Karl Popper's approach to science 'problem' is a key concept. Theories are only means to ends. They are solutions to intellectual problems. We can find problems just as readily in everyday life as we can in science. Some of them are even the same. What is the weather going to be like tomorrow? Why does baby refuse her feed? Even in these mundane cases, everyday life supplies theories to help us act: 'Red sky at night (implies) shepherd's delight'. Statements like this abound and cover every area of our life. To begin to make this statement scientific it needs to obey two rules: first, its corresponding problem must be attached; second, it must be written down. This is so that we can fix it for inspection and avoid interpretations which shift according to the whim of their defenders. It also means we can get at it like a piece of machinery and alter it when it fails.

The significance of this lies in the next requirement which, paradoxically, is that we should now search out where the theory fails. In everyday life theories are constantly tested by experience. Every action we take is the realisation of a belief, and many of these turn out to be wrong. This is where the openness enters into both philosophy and the everyday. Each failed theory constitutes a new problem, and the process starts all over again.

Straight away this view of science throws some light on the validity of science on television and on its implications for the autonomy of the viewer.

First think about validity. Science is a way of thinking and acting that incorporates all of our modes of experience. It needs writing and talk; for its testing, it needs observations and therefore images. All of these television can supply. But science also needs action in the real world. Action in an illusory world is clearly worse than useless: any sort of error or deception could creep through into the argument. Television can only offer illusions of action.

Now turn to autonomy. Which is more scientific: to accept the weather forecaster's prediction and ignore the network of connections and evidence used to produce it? Or to take 'Red sky at night' as a starting point and to have both the technique and the will to adapt it if and when it fails?

Autonomy clearly calls for personal understanding based on the ability to make an explanation which connects with other knowledge one possesses. It is hard to see how this can be achieved without argument, attacking the obvious explanation to find its limits.

Which is more empowering: critical autonomy or specialist information? Undeniably there will be cases when life is too short to re-invent the wheel. The specialist will then be quite useful. But what about the next time, and the next time? Viewed over a life-time as a built-in habit of mind, autonomy must be preferred.

Finally, are there any particular enemies of science and autonomy? Confusion, perhaps? Anything which strips away the means to provide an explanation for oneself? Concealment of the problem? Suppression of the opportunity to find an explanation? Destruction of the individual's resources to make sensible or enlightening decisions?

Where does this put popular television science?

Television and science

Here are some ideas about television science and everyday life which have common currency:

i) Our lives are increasingly permeated by science.

ii) Science is part of our literary culture: television is basically an oral culture.

iii) Most of the science we learn these days comes from television. As we try to make up our mind about them perhaps we should try to maintain the spirit of common sense science. Can we create an argument by constructing explicit counter-statments and then look for experiences which will help us decide?

Is it true that our lives are increasingly permeated by science? There is just as powerful evidence to suggest they are becoming more magical. Think of the way we use a BBC micro to work out our astrology star chart. Or the way the language of science is used as thought-stopping rhetoric rather than explanation. Even the science that enters our lives via technology is increasingly kept at arm's length: 'no user-serviceable parts inside'.

Next, is science a literary culture compared to a basically oral television? Consider each part of the claim. First, it is true that there is a lot of writing in doing science. It helps to keep the argument focused. Yet that does not make science essentially literary. You cannot have science which will not stand up to criticism in debate. But there is a more fundamental point still. Every written theory needs to be interpreted. Talk is an essential tool in the process of getting from written statement to practical decision and back again.

On the face of it the claim that television is essentially an oral form seems a better fit. But at a deeper level the structures of television can be thought of as essentially written structures. Television is not a flexible medium: in fact it can be most recalcitrant. To control it producers have to plan and share those plans in writing. At the point of writing, written structures begin to determine oral performance.

Finally, do we learn most of our science from television? Again, there is some truth in this but given the comment about media and science above the natural question that occurs is: how can we learn any science at all from television?

Television can, however, perform some useful functions. First, it can help us by placing unsuspected problems on our social agenda. It can make explicit emergent problems and problems of which we are dimly aware, but lack the confidence to articulate. This is the crucial first stage to finding theories to solve them. But we must take the responsibility ourselves to choose between the problems it presents.

Television can also present solutions to problems. But watch out for solutions in isolation. Acting on them you might solve the 'wrong' problem; you may be horrified by the follow-on problems your solution creates.

What television cannot do is test. In fact there is a danger that television can make erroneous theories seem 'right' because it essentially deals in illusion. In science, in writing, in television it is theory which is attacked and destroyed by the test. But in everyday life we embody these theories in ourselves, Destruction of a theory threatens, in the mildest case, a practical way of living; in extreme cases, it is that self which is threatened.

Television, however, has other potentials based on its ability to create illusions of relationships. It can encourage those who inhabit the everyday world that the scientists and the television science presenter are in there with us, and not in Dr Faustus' workshop. In this way it could offer a model of science in growth, being changed, held to be provisional. To succeed it needs to make demands of the viewer to reflect and at the same time encourage us with questions to answer for ourselves. We might suggest that success or failure in this respect is a criterion for *The Real World*.

At its best television science helps people to lead a better life, to be more interested in their world, to understand it better and to be anxious to share that understanding. But any good can be seized as a mask to conceal other purposes. Images of science can be used to promote ways of thinking intrinsically hostile to science and to personal autonomy. It is not just that television can show us something 'before our very eyes' when it is an illusion. Its worst failing is to prevent us from thinking through explanations and even keeping the need for them off the agenda. At such moments science on television does not just look like the magic of the music hall. It has become what real magicians do. Then science on television is not science at all. It is a magic which confuses and ultimately oppresses. As Isaac Asimov comments: 'the difference to the public between a scientist and a magician is the difference between understanding and not understanding and that is also the difference between respect and admiration on the one side, and hate and fear on the other.'

Neil Ryder

REPRESENTATION

What makes a scientific issue?

Representation is a slippery term, particularly in the field of television. The following account of its main connotations, by Richard Dyer, is the clearest and most succinct available. It provides an excellent outline to the concerns of the three chapters which follow in this section of the book:

> We can distinguish four different connotations of the term, each of considerable importance. First, representation suggests re-presentation, presenting reality over again to us. It is often said that television is a 'window on the world', transparent and unmediated; and it is equally often said that it is nothing of the sort, that it is pure fabrication. The notion of representation can get us out of this empty opposition by focusing on the way television actively makes sense of a world that none the less exists separately from television. 'Representation' insists that there is a real world, but that our perception of it is always mediated by television's selection, emphasis and use of technical/aesthetic means to render that world to us.
>
> Equally there is no perception of the world except one that is mediated through the forms of representation available in the culture, of which television is one of the most powerful. The notion of representation keeps open that tension between television images themselves and the reality that those images *make* sense of. What is politically at stake here is *what* sense they make of the world, not the inescapable fact that they do so.
>
> Secondly, 'representation' suggests the function of 'being representative of'. In other words, it raises the question of *typicality.* To what extent are representations of men and women, whites and blacks, different classes, etc. typical of how those groups are in society? All communication must deal in the typical. We cannot communicate only through the utterly unique, particular and individuated. It is unhelpful to fall into the position . . . that considers stereotypes as *necessarily* derogatory. What matters is not *that* we have typical representations on television, but rather *what* they are, what harm they do to the well-being of the groups that they represent.
>
> Thirdly, there is representation in the sense implied in the Representation of the People Act, that is, in the sense of *speaking for and on behalf of.* This is where the most political heat is generated

because, faced with television images, we constantly need to ask not 'What is this image of?' so much as 'Who is speaking here?'. For every image of a woman, it is important to ask who is speaking for women at that point. In the vast majority of cases, the answer would be a man. The same is true of other groups excluded from the mainstream of speech in our society. Television so often speaks on our behalf without letting us speak for ourselves.

Finally, representation should also make us think of the *audience*. In this inflection, we should include ourselves: what does this programme represent to me; what does it mean to other people who watch it? We often leave this stage out of account; especially, I regret to say, in education. Teachers often try to get pupils and students to see what a programme represents 'ideally' (i.e. as *teachers* understand it) without also finding out what it represents to them. We need to learn to listen better – especially to children – to understand what sense they in turn make out of the work represented to them.

Questions that teachers can debate with their pupils stem readily from these different connotations of the term representation. What sense of the world is this programme making? What does it claim is typical of the world and what deviant? Who is really speaking? For whom? What does it represent to us, and why?

(Lusted & Drummond, 1985, pp. 41–6)

Dyer's fourth sense of representation focuses on audiences and in particular on the interactions between audiences and programmes. We shall be examining this more fully in the final section of the book. This section will concentrate on the three other senses of representation.

A further perspective on representation, which draws attention to the specific characteristics of television, is offered by John Ellis:

Broadcast TV has a particular regime of representation that stresses the immediacy and co-presence of the TV representation. Its particular physical and social characteristics have created a very particular mode of representation that includes the image centred upon the significant at the cost of detail, and sound as carrier of continuity. It gives its audience a particular sense of intimacy with the events it portrays.

(Ellis, 1982, p. 137)

1

Studying *The Real World*

Television truth
Asking questions
Making connections?
Magic and reality
The go-betweens
A seamless flow
The uncertain scientist

> Television opens windows. It says there is a view on life which you probably thought you could never take part in, you could never bring yourself to enjoy because it's beyond you. Television says "Here, have a go, you can do it!"
>
> Michael Rodd, Presenter, *The Real World*

All media use some kind of symbolic system to represent reality. Some, like writing, use systems whose symbols are markedly different in appearance from the phenomena they represent. Others, like television or photography, use symbols which are apparently more 'realistic': they claim implicitly to reflect the world rather than to refract it.

One of television's most commonly cited features is its ability vividly to reproduce the world as we know it. It offers us a transparent means of observation, a 'window on the world'. It not only shows the world to be clearly and reassuringly *there*, but also seems to persuade us that what we are witnessing is an accurate and reliable representation of that world. It promises us, as *The Real World*'s title implies, an objective perspective on the physical and social world which we all inhabit.

Does it necessarily follow that viewers are deluded by television's realistic mode? Does its ability to create illusions mean that it is dishonest? To what extent do viewers collude with the conventions of television and help to sustain its illusions?

This chapter provides some starting points for examining television's habitual means of representation and its familiar symbolic systems more closely and more critically.

Television truth

Television images are usually considerably smaller than the reality they represent. They are also, unlike their originals, two-dimensional. In spite of these real differences, television creates the illusion that we are experiencing an actual event rather than a representation. But we need to be wary of metaphors which suggest that we can see the world transparently through television or that it faithfully reflects our own images back to us.

Even if the event *is* actually happening 'live' before the cameras, it is still being represented through a particular viewpoint. Whether the events are live or pre-recorded, concerned with past, present or future, they will still appear to be more 'real' to us on television than they would, say, in a magazine, This is largely because

- television 'translates' events into sounds and images using life-like symbolic systems

- the means of representation (microphones, cameras and crew) are excluded from the action.

This does not mean that we necessarily believe what we see on television to be true. Nor does it mean that television deliberately distorts the truth. It does mean that we cannot expect television (or any other medium, for that matter) to be truthful in this simple sense. As Roger Silverstone points out in his study of a *Horizon* programme:

> in the arrangement of the image, in the reshooting, in the intervention of the director and the cameraman to place and to move elements within the frame, according to some unspecified and perhaps unconscious rhetoric, ⟨images⟩ have to speak and to emphasise an aspect of that reality which is claimed to be significant. There is no fraudulence here, and it should not be misunderstood. It cannot be otherwise. (Silverstone, 1985, p. 77)

But we *can* expect television to try to be truthful in the sense of being valid. We can only assess this at a given moment by understanding

– its means of representation
– its codes and conventions.

Understanding how television works and how viewers respond to what they watch may enable us to exploit its potential more fully. As Umberto Eco says, 'if you want to use television for teaching somebody something, you have first to teach somebody how to use television' (*Screen Education 31*, 1979, p. 15). With this in mind, we shall be raising basic questions about how television represents the world – questions which are important to us all. For, if we want to understand the world, we need first of all to know not only what we are looking at, but also how, why and through what lenses.

Asking questions

Why study a programme like *The Real World*? It is hardly typical of broadcast television – but it must be acknowledged that it is not easy to find one which is. One reason is that it is a kind of programme which has been rarely studied in the past. Another is that, as a science programme, it deals with areas of human knowledge which are widely recognized as being of vital importance to us all (as the Royal Society's report on science education reminds us). The way in which it deals with its subject-matter is also of great general interest. For above all, like much of television, it tells stories.

Investigating how it chose and shaped the stories which it tells is rather like some of the scientific processes which *The Real World* itself features. Studying *Dead as the Dodo?* is a kind of archaeological enterprise. We have the general detritus of massive amounts of documentary evidence whose survival seems sometimes haphazard and accidental. We have major fossil remains in the form of memos, notes and scripts. Their genealogy has helped us to chart the evolution of the finished programme.

We also have the live testimony of the main participants in the production process who have been able to fill in the gaps where necessary. Interviews with them have helped us to retrieve and interpret the surviving information. As with any historical account, we have had to select from the material available to us and to apply knowledge from other sources where appropriate. Given the starting-point of the project our research has also been mostly retrospective. We do, however, have the programme itself and this provides the richest resource for examining its own dynamics.

Our approach concentrates on three major questions which could usefully be asked of any science programme on television. These questions have also led us into investigating what is distinctive about *The Real World*. They provide the underlying framework for this book.

- What makes a scientific issue?
- How are scientific issues presented?
- How do audiences respond?

What makes the programme so interesting to us (and therefore we expect to others) is its oddity. This is not just a matter of its sometimes quirky choice of topics, or its interest in fringe science, the paranormal or extra-terrestrial intelligence. Nor is it the cheeky tone with which it often approaches scientific issues. *The Real World* is unusual because it is produced by a Regional ITV company and runs as a short series of only seven programmes annually; and it is also interesting because the audiences it seems to speak to are not the ones who actually watch it.

Some disparity between assumed and actual audiences is not unusual. 18% of the *Grange Hill* audience consists of people over 55 years old and 3 million of its 5.5 million regular viewers have already left school. Similarly, *Dangermouse*, although watched by 1 million of its preferred 4–9 year old audience, is watched by nearly 1.5 million viewers over 55.

Making connections?

The Real World strives within each programme to make connections between disparate scientific discoveries, but will sometimes fail to make the connections between its own programmes. For example, *Dead as the Dodo?*, which is essentially concerned with the origins of life and the possibilities of creating it artificially, invokes Fred Hoyle's theory of the extra-terrestrial origin of human life by accidental meteorite contact with the Earth. This theory depends crucially on the notion of animal tissues from another planet surviving a cosmic journey. A year later, a programme in a new series of *The Real World* which deals with the possibility of extra-terrestrial intelligence returns to the question of what it calls 'the foundations of life itself'. The same clip of meteorite film is used again. Yet nowhere is there any reference to the earlier programme or even an apparent awareness of its existence.

Similarly, a later programme in the 1985 series, *Body – Can You Spare a Part?* is concerned with the giving of life through transplant surgery. The ethical issues discussed in that programme are even more acutely relevant to the problem of cloning raised in the *Dead as the Dodo?* programme but are not even mentioned in it. Nor is there any connection made in the educational 'back-up' material. This is by no means unusual for such series. And perhaps it need not be considered strictly necessary to achieve such continuity.

What can we make of this kind of discontinuity between programmes in the same series? One approach is to look at the production and distribution processes. First of all, the programmes and their educational 'back-up' are consciously and inevitably separate. They were handled by different departments in TVS, and have quite different aims and different audiences. Further, within the producing department (Factual Programmes) there were three different producers, two of whom were responsible for the programmes mentioned above. There were also three researchers involved in the 1985 series with responsibilities for different programmes. Although there was an Executive Producer from TVS' permanent staff, many of the producers and researchers were freelance employees who only worked together for six months during the research, production and transmission of a single series of programmes. In addition, there was little continuity of scientific expertise either from the permanent staff or through the use of consultants.

Referring to specific production constraints, however, deals with only half of the problem. This kind of discontinuity is almost a general characteristic of television. It is a problem which is familiar in news programmes, where long-running events fall out of the agenda when their peak of interest has passed and lapse into a kind of limbo world. It happens, too, in popular serials where certain events have to be 'forgotten' to make way for alternative futures. One thinks of Bobby's resurrection to save the *Dallas* ratings.

It is somehow part of the experience of television viewing, related in an obvious way to its immediacy, its 'nowness'. The pace of presentation is often breathless. *Dead as the Dodo?* has an average shot-length of only six seconds, which may cause it to achieve local colour and contrast at the expense of general clarity or firmly structured argument. As Garfield Kennedy, producer of *Dead as the Dodo?*, explains:

> 'if you look at a programme and you feel that it's just flat and all the same, I feel that you've probably failed in a *Real World*. It shouldn't be one simple idea strung across for twenty-six minutes, it's got to be kind of choppy and bumpy and almost uncomfortable'.

Given this need for pace and variety, even expert scientists are subjected to rigorous editing. It is not unusual for any documentary programme to use less that 10% of originally recorded interview material. But in *Dead as the Dodo?* the 'talking heads' sequences are reduced even further. Of nine interview sequences in the programme, the longest is eighty seconds and the mean average is twenty-five seconds.

Another way of explaining the programme's style is to relate it to what is normally expected of television audiences and to what audiences expect of television. Ever since the work of Goodhart and Ehrenberg, it has been clear that the composition of audiences for all but the most compelling series and serials changes drastically from week to week. Gross viewing figures may remain similar from one programme to another in the series. But only about half of the audience for a specific programme is carried forward to the next one. This kind of 'exponential decay' occurs in classic form with *The Real World*. In the 1986 series, for example, 46% of all adult viewers watching television at the time saw programme 1. Only 21% saw programme 2 as well. Less than 1% saw all seven in the series. It is now also becoming increasingly evident that the attention which audiences give to television is seldom total and often competes with a range of other domestic demands. These factors exert a powerful influence on the content, shape and style of the programme. They also provide limits to the kind of connections which can be made within and between the different programmes in a series.

Magic and reality

The Real World is a title which makes large claims. These claims are extended through the programme's publicity and 'back-up' materials with their emphasis on how science affects people's lives. In Michael Rodd's words, it aims to 'take the magical things that people do in laboratories and discuss the effect they are going to have on you and me. Our aim has always been to make a science programme which made sense to everbody in the real world.'

The use of the word 'magical' in this context seems far from innocent; nor is Michael Rodd's avowed objective as straightforward as he would like to make out. As Roger Silverstone suggests, 'Science and television have different ways of speaking and of addressing the world. Both use words and pictures to be sure but one is firmly grounded in literary culture and the other, perhaps less stably, is grounded in an oral one' (Silverstone, 1985, p. 163). As a result, when television producers expect forms of communication from scientists which are appropriate to the demands of the medium, they are effectively putting communication skills before expertise in scientific research. This problem is addressed in *The Real World* by using the presenters as entrepreneurs between the world of science and the world of television.

But there is another potential conflict in a programme like *The Real World*. Although it is not strictly an educational programme, it clearly has educative pretensions. It is also earmarked by the IBA as a programme with a specific educational role. There is, as a result, a tension between, on the one hand, its desire to inform and educate and, on the other, its need to entertain, scheduled as it was at 7pm on a Monday.

This tension often produces an uncertain, sometimes nervous, relationship with audiences. For the *The Real World* this manifests itself in an eagerness, even an anxiety to please. Some critics such as Gardner and Young argue that as a result, 'Science broadcasting is "educating" viewers in one sense – about the nature of scientific progress – while firmly keeping them in the role of school children in relation to visual and critical sophistication' (Bennett *et al.*, 1981, p. 179). Sometimes the apparently straightforward promise of making sense to Michael Rodd's audience of 'everybody in the real world' is unfulfilled because programmes do not make sense of the issues beneath the surface. It must certainly be difficult to reconcile the aim of making sense with the constant shifts of attention from cloning or artificial insemination to extra-terrestrial intelligence and prehistoric apes.

But it is not just in its title, or in publicity about the programme, that this promise of insight into 'the real world' is offered. It is built into its very texture. (Even the use of one female and one male presenter may be seen as an attempt to reflect naïvely the real world of gender.) Its narrative creates a particular blend of studio links and exposition, on the one hand, with film-location visits and interviews, on the other. At another level, the studio provides a kind of back-cloth which helps to frame and familiarise the programme's excursions into the unusual and unknown. Its artful presentation represents the 'magic' of the laboratory.

The go-betweens

The role of the presenters is that of benevolent and enthusiastic guides around the exciting world of scientific discoveries. By means of their personal 'magic', we can accept that the real world is both challengingly 'out there' on the frontiers of knowledge and reassuringly 'here' in the comfortable solidity of the studio, where programmes invariably return for their finale. Sometimes an impressive fusion occurs between the cosy intimacy of the studio and the public world beyond its boundaries. Where private and public worlds meet, in laboratories and studies, scientists quietly pursue their goals. The presenter is, as Robins and Webster claim, 'the user-friendly expert. He or she is the public relations expert, the sales rep. for the scientific, technological and industrial establishment. To him or her falls the task of giving the human touch to abstract and complex issues, of dressing up science and technology for public consumption' (Masterman, 1984, p. 112).

But this role is not confined to popular science programmes. The relationship between presenter and programme actually has a market value outside the programme itself. In advertisements and in corporate video, many of these same voices and faces reappear persuading audiences into certain attitudes or even purchasing decisions. As Philip Simpson explains:

> Once a personality and a programme create an image, the meanings of that image can be sold and be set in play in other

contexts: Sue Pollard and *Hi-de-Hi!* created an image that helps to sell tea, but what meanings did *Monty Python, Fawlty Towers* and John Cleese create together so that his image can be used to sell computers and the SDP?   (Jones, 1986)

The presenter therefore creates an image of power, trust and authority based on charisma and personality. But that is only half the story. It is certainly the 'preferred reading' but it does not take into account the reactions of audiences.

The very fact that such figures are to be found in other persuasive contexts like advertisements may actually reduce their power in absolute terms. How can you trust someone who is enthusing about a *Tomorrow's World* gadget one minute if they're trying to sell you a new car the next?

In some cases, the assertion of power may itself be so frontal for an audience that it causes the role of presenter to self-destruct. The 'hard sell' can be self-defeating, as Clive James found with James Burke's programme *The Real Thing*:

> What James Burke can't seem to grasp is that I don't care about not possessing the information he has. It is a matter of total indifference whether he is the way he looks – i.e., the right way up and practically exploding with pedagogic enthusiasm, or whether he is upside down, plugged into an electric socket, and all set to eat a live chicken. But there is no way of telling him this, because instead of being an actual presence you can reach out towards and beat repeatedly around the head with a rolled-up newspaper until you get his attention, he is an image on your television screen that goes on and on supplying you with information you don't have. Merely turning the programme off is no good, since the after-image lingers on. You have to kick the set in even to slow him down.
>
> (James, 1983, p. 71)

The presenter's role may also be to act as host when a scientist is brought into the studio, as in the case of Dr Phil Laipis in *Dead as the Dodo?* It is rare, however, for this form of traffic to occur. More frequently, the cameras, crew and presenters 'discover' the scientists in their 'natural' environment. Their journey provides an accessible parallel with the work of scientists, involving viewers in the process of observation, investigation and interrogation.

A seamless flow

Cohesion is often achieved quite subtly, however, by means of gentle narrative transitions. Towards the end of *Dead as the Dodo?*, for example, the presenter Michael Rodd is found on location. There, he explains how a fruit-fly became trapped in amber 23 million years ago in a rain-forest in the Dominican Republic. The final shot of the location sequence comes to rest on the hardened resin of a near-by tree.

The transition to the next interview begins by means of a visual mix to a close-up of a fruit-fly encased in amber. The camera zooms in gently and the shot mixes again to another fruit-fly close-up, panning down slowly as it does so. While this is happening, Michael Rodd's voice-over introduces us verbally to Dr George Poinar at Berkeley. Poinar's voice glides in gently over the second fruit-fly close-up as the camera continues its pan down. The sequence cuts to a head-and-shoulders shot of Poinar speaking against a background of books as he smoothly develops the sentence begun over the shot of the fruit-fly. He speaks for sixteen seconds before the visual track cuts to a different fruit-fly specimen. As he continues to explain their scientific value, yet another visual mix takes us to the microbiological level of cellular structure and finally back to a mid-shot of Poinar sitting with his fruit-fly specimens displayed on a desk beside him.

1   2

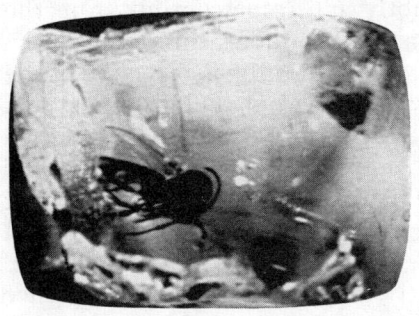

3

4

5

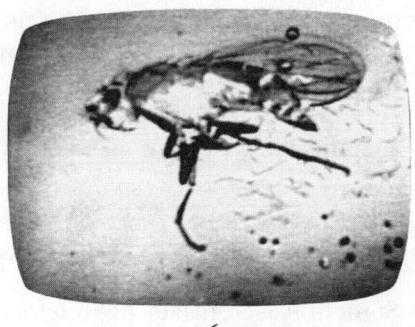

6

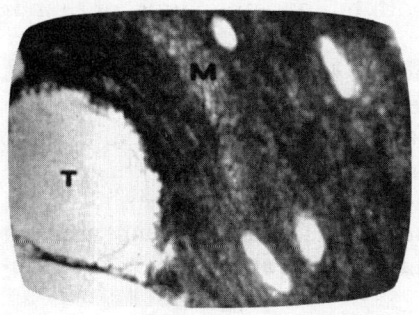

7

8

In this way, we have moved subtly and imperceptibly from the presenter on location in the natural environment, through the outward appearance of the specimens, to the framing perspective of the scientist and down to the microscopic level of their composition. This is the 'seamless flow' of television narrative. It makes a fascinating comparison with the unevenness of actual scientific work, and of the process of filming itself. Michael Rodd is not in fact in the Dominican Republic, as the viewer might imagine, but in San Diego Zoo, the home of animal specimens frozen by Dr Oliver Ryder.

The filming process was exactly the reverse of the sequence as viewed. It was, in fact, much more opportunist. It began with the producer in Poinar's office in Berkeley, continued with the visit to San Diego Zoo and was concluded when a suitable resinated tree was found there. This then became the back-cloth for Michael Rodd's link to take the viewer back to Poinar's Berkeley office. Such subtle transitions are both smooth and apparently effortless, and they have a cumulative effect in constructing the particular synthetic reality of *The Real World.* The telescoping of time and place creates a texture for the programme which fixes a specific view of man as scientist, shaking hands with nature.

The uncertain scientist

Somehow scientists on television seem to have a conviction and self-confidence in their manner which we encounter only rarely in our daily experience. Obviously, they have the luxury of being filmed through several 'takes' in order to put their ideas clearly and incisively. They also enjoy the benefit of an editing process which has a vested interest in creating a smooth but dynamic 'flow' of sounds and images.

But such smoothness and satisfaction are only achieved at a price. There is a tendency throughout the production of *The Real World* to close off some issues which might otherwise remain open, to elide areas of uncertainty or possible confusion. At one level, this may be inevitable, as transmission deadlines approach. At another, it may be argued that the viewer requires and the medium itself encourages a finale which achieves some sort of reassuring and satisfying equilibrium.

The problems begin when such certainty covers up the mysteries and doubts which are inherent in scientific processes. For example, when George Poinar was asked by Michael Rodd in Berkeley whether he was confident that DNA in the amber was viable, his actual answer was hesitant and uncertain:

> 'Well, I can't say I'm confident in there but I think there's a chance that it could be viable and that's why we're progressing with this. We think there's a good chance because it looks very nice.'

The answer which was subsequently used in the edited programme was the result of a supplementary question from Michael Rodd based on a hypothesis supplied by the presenter himself:

> RODD   But suppose that it is ⟨viable⟩, aren't you simply going to end up confirming what you know already, rather than taking our understanding forward in any particular direction?
>
> POINAR   Well, if we found that it was viable this would open up a new chapter because no one really believes that DNA can be viable for such a long period. So we wouldn't confirm anything that we already knew . . .

Poinar's answer to Michael Rodd's final question, about the possibility of life having originated somewhere else than on this planet, is a far cry from the genial confidence which Poinar displays in the edited programme:

> 'Well it gives the probability and the possibility of this occurring because it doesn't say that it could (*sic*) there might have been a mixture of life starting here on this planet, but it opens the possibility of life coming from other sources, when I'm speaking, I'm now speaking about life and at this point still speaking about microbial forms of life, spores and things like this, fungal and bacterial spores. And, uh, this could be mixed with different sources, or it could be mixed with what was here, what originated here and it's all very interesting because the more you look into it the less you see we really understand about it all.'

There is nothing dishonest or fraudulent in such elisions. It is, as the earlier quotation from Silverstone suggested, an inevitable consequence of the production process. Such transformations, however, do offer an insight into how television works.

To study this programme is to address some of the most fundamental issues in an understanding of television. For, in the end, the programme is partly about television itself. Not only does it constantly remind us of its televisuality through its use of visual effects, but it reinforces it verbally as well. There is even a whole programme in the 1985 series, *Behind the Lines*, devoted to developments in screen technology. The most powerful example of this reflexivity comes at the very end of the 1986 programme, *Hello?* on the possibility of extra-terrestrial intelligence. Here, in the final shot of the programme, we are invited to eavesdrop on an unidentified alien who sits with her back to us observing life on Earth. Her means of surveillance is not a radio telescope but, perhaps inevitably, a television.

2
Science Fact and Fiction

Science on television
Scientific viewpoints
The courage to question

Television and science have their own languages. They each make their own demands on their audience – demands which are often in competition with each other. This chapter explores the tensions within television science, between its need to entertain and its mission to educate.

In our everyday lives we are constantly asked to make decisions and judgements which are based on scientific knowledge. Where does this knowledge come from? Does television offer anything to help us? What kind of aims and assumptions do television science producers have? What conclusions can be drawn about the role of science in our culture?

Science on television

Both Garfield Kennedy, in talking about *The Real World*, and Roger Silverstone, in observing the making of a BBC *Horizon* programme, comment upon the way a story develops. It may depend upon how much the participants conform to the expectations of television producers. Silverstone describes a producer's disappointment over his key figure's inability to communicate effectively on camera. He was forced to change the emphasis of the story because he had to find a televisual personality good enough to carry the science. The original story may also have to accommodate new developments. Garfield Kennedy and Michael Rodd both comment on the definite shift which occurred in the *Dodo* programme while they were filming in San Diego. Telephone calls from England convinced them that they must develop the human genealogy element in the story more fully. At the same time, they were both very anxious about one of their 'star' scientists who did not come over well on film. This led eventually to the inclusion of the Gainesville skull sequence, the studio interview with the team's representative, Dr Phil Laipis, and a drastic reduction in screen time for the less articulate scientist. What factors motivated these changes?

One factor relates to producers' conceptions of their audiences. Alec Nisbett, a BBC Science Features producer, divides audiences into three types: 'The largest group of viewers are those with little or no knowledge of science, followed by a much smaller group with some scientific training but limited direct knowledge, and finally a very small group of specialists who work in a particular field of science' (Nisbett, 1984, p. 15). Producers of science programmes targeted at mass audiences tend to regard their viewers as ignorant about science, and their programmes maintain a perspective on science which does not generally encourage doubt, exploration or argument. Do they, as one critic recently put it, lack 'the courage to be boring'?

The differences in style and format between television science programmes reflect their relationship to their audiences. At one end of the spectrum, Open University broadcasts are often presented in a form similar to a lecture. At the other end, *Tomorrow's World* is made up of a series of short items which focus on new gadgets and inventions, many of which are only on the periphery of science. *Tomorrow's World* calls upon the viewer to marvel at technology's new tricks. Garfield Kennedy acknowledges the power of such an approach when he refers to the tactics of maintaining audience attention by bringing in 'gosh! factors', as opposed to 'yawn factors'.

In between educational and popular science lies the 'serious' science programme, of which *Horizon* is the perfect example. Alongside it must also be set documentaries such as *TV Eye* and *Panorama* with their occasional investigations into the political dimensions of scientific issues. Serious science concentrates on one main issue and develops an argument around it. Unlike popular science, there is greater emphasis placed on ideas. This often means that the role of the presenter is less significant. In most *Horizon* programmes, voice-over is used to link the argument together and present a coherent overview.

Science as
Enlightenment

Science as
Entertainment

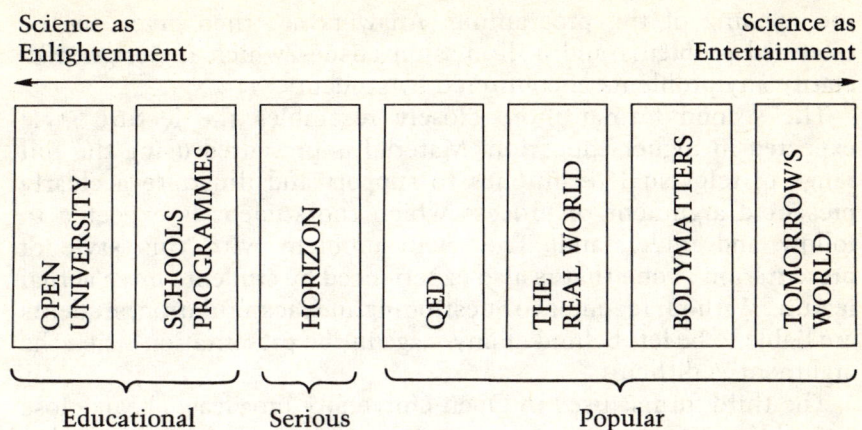

Educational	Serious	Popular

Serious science programmes are aimed at an audience which has some knowledge of science. Most programmes in this category are documentary in style, and the level of language used presupposes an audience familiar with science. This may make the programmes inaccessible to mass audiences.

Serious science programmes do not attract the same size of audience as popular science programmes, and they tend to be broadcast on BBC2 after the peak-viewing period. *Horizon* was moved to an earlier evening slot in the schedules in an attempt to secure a larger audience. They are also typically longer than other forms of actuality science on television. *Horizon* and 'blockbuster' natural history series like *Life on Earth* are usually 50 minutes to an hour long.

The range of educational science programming, including Schools broadcasts and the Open University, is greater than can be discussed here. The Open University alone produces over 900 hours of material which can be grouped into four main categories, each adopting a different format and requiring different responses from its audience.

The first uses a format not found in general broadcasting, nor in other types of educational broadcasting and is quite different from the 'lecture to camera' format. It requires the viewer to undertake a high degree of activity during transmission. Following an introduction to the topic in question, viewers become involved in a number of exercises which they solve by reference to the material presented in the opening of the programme. Answers are then given to the televised problems and a discussion ensues which is designed to clarify any problems encountered by students.

The second format more closely resembles the lecture style expected in higher education. Material is presented using the full range of televisual techniques to support and illustrate a clearly presented argument or process which the student is expected to follow and understand. The main problem with this style of presentation is one that is also experienced by students in an actual lecture. Without recourse to questioning and racapitulation, students are liable to be left behind at any stage in the presentation when the argument is difficult.

The third format used in Open University broadcasts bears close resemblance to programmes found in the general broadcast schedules. It provides students with a specific kind of experience, such as a dramatic performance or an introduction to a new topic in a format similar to a conventional documentary such as the BBC's *Horizon* series. At least part of this type of Open University broadcast is aimed at feelings, attitudes and ideological perspectives. Often it is the process of reaching a better understanding of such material which is as important as the range of actual conclusions students might reach as they watch the programme or reflect upon it afterwards. This format presents problems for viewers. The programmes tend to be seen as interesting and enjoyable to watch but of little value except as 'glossy extras' to the course. Some students are frustrated by the lack of clear 'correct' questions and answers in the material presented. They feel the need to be participants rather than mere spectators.

The fourth format used in Open University broadcasts presents similar problems for students. The case-study, or film of natural events, encourages students to make links between the film and the rest of the course material. Since students recognise this format as one met in general broadcasting, they may be seduced into considering it as a 'soft option', requiring little learning response on their part. They associate general broadcasts with leisure and entertainment rather than learning.

Educational and serious programmes are fairly clearly indentifiable. The term 'popular', however, raises all sorts of problems. The various studies which focus on popular television refer mainly to audience size or appeal, or to a recognisable style of presentation. The question which has not been answered is: what makes a programme which is popular in the latter sense also popular in the former? It is also clear that popular was once a term of abuse but has now become (particularly as a result of recent work on 'soap opera') almost an academic qualification. More specifically, it seems to be used with some or all of the following characteristics in mind:

- recurrent, or serial, showing
- transmission in peak-time viewing
- large national audiences (over about 4 million)
- familiar currency in everyday discourse or gossip
- regular features and comment in the tabloid press
- presence of 'stars' and personalities
- specific presentational codes and conventions (e.g. naturalism, fast cutting)
- formulaic plots or formats
- elements of redundancy linked with level of audience attention (monitoring or skimming by viewers)
- elements of fantasy linked with audience aspirations
- invitation to identify with characters
- recognisable forms of audience pleasure (suspense, fulfilment, surprise)
- ideologically normative and consensual

It is perhaps because of the frequent linkage of pleasure with escapism that popular television has often been dismissed as 'mere entertainment'. There is certainly a distaste for, and even fear of, the popular in the 1983 DES Report on *Popular Television and Schoolchildren*. As Richard Dyer comments: 'What is entertaining about *Tomorrow's World* is the way that it constructs a tomorrow for today's world to escape into via the unproblematic, colourful, jaunty use of technology. The core of *Tomorrow's World*'s appeal is just as much escapism as *Top of the Pops*' (Lusted & Drummond, 1985, p. 42). Dyer is concerned to investigate and recognise the sources of pleasure which we find in popular television and suggests that they derive from certain kinds of visual appeal and a confirmation of the familiar and the consensual.

Alan Coren, television critic for *The Mail on Sunday* also addresses the question of pleasure in popular science programmes when writing about BBC programmes screened in February 1987. He focuses on humour:

Levity is the only mode for science programmes. There is no other way of attracting a scientifically illiterate audience, and since that is the only kind of audience there is, television has to take the facts and wrap them up in giggles.

The standard levity pattern derives from the Hammer Film, i.e., you bring a crackpot into contact with something horrible. The crackpot can be Heinz Wolff, David Bellamy, Magnus Pyke, or anyone else with a peculiar voice and hysterical hands, and the best kind of horrible thing is one that eats you.

(*Mail on Sunday*, 8 Feb 1987, p. 35)

This view is echoed by Karl Sabbagh, director of *The Living Body* for Channel 4:

Being made to laugh, particularly in unexpected contexts, is a useful means of getting audience sympathy and interest . . . it depends on people getting some sort of enjoyment out of their viewing. That enjoyment can come from making discoveries, for example, or having curiosity aroused or seeing some beautiful pictures, or being made aware of something about yourself you didn't know before.

(*See 4*, 14, p. 33).

Science programmes in this category aim at a mass audience with little or no knowledge of science. Whereas serious science programmes like *Horizon* may expect an audience of between two and five million each week, the popular science programme will aim to capture an audience of eight to ten million. This is partly a reflection of its position in the broadcast schedules but it is also related to the programme format and style.

The style of programme in this category is perhaps its most distinctive feature. Aubrey Singer, the creator of *Tomorrow's World*, is reported to have said that the response he desired was an awed 'Gee whizz!', from the viewer after every item. But, as Robins and Webster explain, this philosophy has its flip-side:

Tomorrow's World sets out to fascinate, to surprise, to astonish and amaze. It is a shop window regaled with sleek new inventions and technological toys. But the consequence of this gee-whiz enthusiasm for new technological developments is to present a vision of the future which is no more than a bad infinity of gadgets and devices and one that leaves us feeling saturated, jaded and even apathetic. Like a junk cereal, it's unsustaining. *Only* snap, crackle and pop. We become, after a while, inoculated against any feelings of surprise or anticipation, so that the future comes to seem, paradoxically, *un*exciting.   (Masterman, 1984, p. 11)

Science's use of specialised terms and names is a major obstacle to popular presentation, and the language used in the popular science programme takes into account the audience's lack of scientific knowledge. Most of these specialised terms are 'definition-loaded': that is they have very precise meanings to the specialist, and their use is vital for effective communication between scientists. Without access to the precise meaning of these terms, the layman will struggle to communicate effectively with scientists. The role of popular science presenters, therefore, is that of interpreter between the specialist and the layman. Their role is to de-mystify the science and remove the cloak of secrecy provided by scientific terminology. To scientists the alternative language will seem crude and imprecise, but it is the only way the layman can gain access to the scientists' domain. One obvious consequence of this popular form of science programming is the development of particular stereotypes about science which congeal into pervasive ideologies. Modern science is seen as the purveyor of technological solutions to human problems. The ideology of scientism, as Dunn puts it, has flourished:

> This ideology pervades contemporary thought in business, education and politics, justifying exploitative conditions in the economy, confining specialisations in higher learning and repressive measures on the part of Government. Bound exclusively to technical criteria, scientism represents a closed universe of discourse, where alternatives to prevailing societal arrangements are automatically dismissed by restricting definitions of reality to the existing factual order. The hidden nucleus of scientism, however, is manipulation and control, where the domination of people is inseparable from and justified by 'the management of things'. Indeed, the major function of the ideology of scientism is to disguise its domination as a series of technical solutions called for by 'scientific expertise'.
>   (Dunn, 1979, p. 343)

A similar complaint is made by Robins and Webster:

> The achievement of this powerful myth – of this scientism – is to effectively depoliticise, dehistoricise and desocialise our understanding of science and technology. Repressed is any awareness of those forces that constitute the technologies to express their own narrow and particular values and priorities: nuclear corporations; pharmaceutical companies; electronics and aerospace interests; police and military agencies. No mention of transnational corporations, of capital and of profit making. No mention of the relations of power that in reality shape and inform the supposedly neutral realm of science and technology. Nowhere is it suggested that technology grinds people down in factories, that it leads to ecological devastation and pollution, or that it may now threaten even our very survival. Within this discursive realm, in Barthes' words, 'A conjuring trick has taken place: it has turned reality inside out, it has emptied it of history and has filled it with nature . . .
>
> (Masterman, 1984, p. 112)

Some critics find the ideologies of popular television in general and popular television science in particular worthy of suspicion. The pleasure it offers to many people is undeniable. What causes concern is the underlying philosophy.

Where *The Real World* fits in

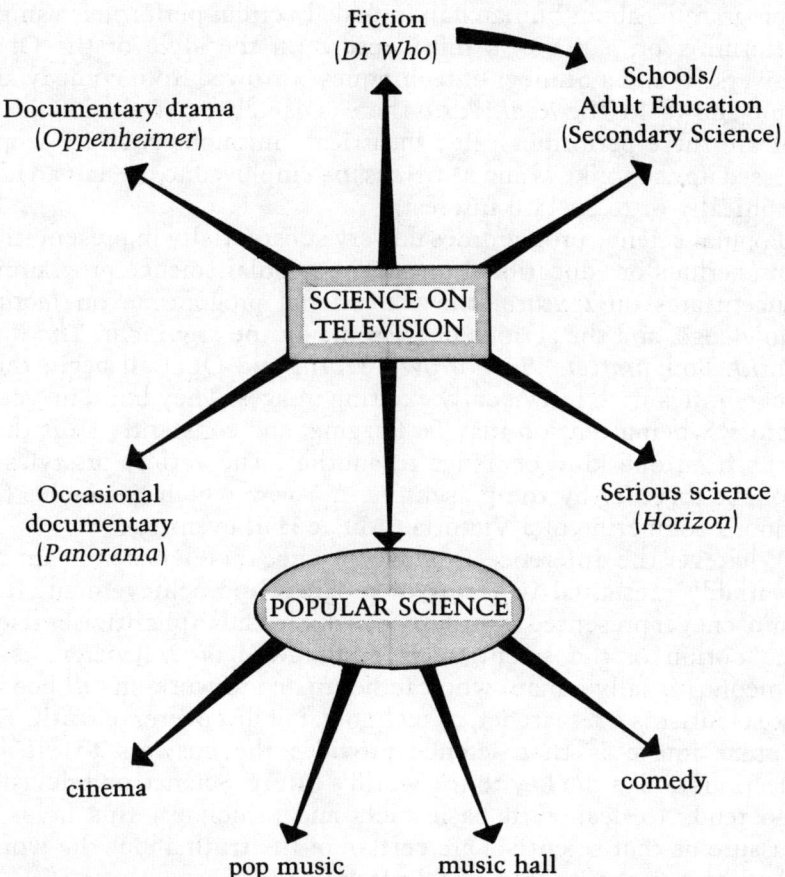

Scientific viewpoints

Although science programmes differ in content, many stylistic features are 'borrowed' not only from each other but from other areas of television and theatre. All science programmes, even *Horizon* at its most serious, rely on a particular kind of visual rhetoric. As Roger Silverstone puts it: 'Convertible images allow the reality of the unfamiliar, the new, the different, the beautiful or the ugly to be communicated effectively.' (Silverstone 1985, p. 64).

Bodymatters, the popular medical science programme, has adopted the format of a cabaret or night-club. The studio audience sits around tables and the programme presenters move from one table to another. A programme about human hair included a circus performer, a singer performing on a piano, a mini-lecture (in the style of the Open University) and a number of techniques borrowed from comedy and game-shows. In *The Real World* there is usually no studio audience, nor are there performers. But theatrical gimmicks such as people dressed up as monkeys and Martians *are* employed to present an idea graphically or to sustain interest.

Popular science programmes do vary substantially in presentation from serious or educational ones. The popular science programme concentrates on *texture*; the educational programme on *factual knowledge*, and the serious programme on the *argument*. *The Real World*, *Bodymatters*, *Tomorrow's World* and *QED* all begin their programmes with televisually exciting images. They build in 'gosh! factors' when attention may be flagging, and constantly shift their focus from one kind of image to another. The variety of styles is brought together by the presenters in a way which resembles the smooth compèring of a Victorian Music Hall evening.

Whatever the differences, though, science on television is almost invariably presented in terms of progress and achievement. It is almost never presented as an activity which doubts or criticises itself. The notion of the scientist, as pronounced on television, is of someone (usually a man) who can be trusted to work on *our* behalf: the scientist is a researcher, or technocrat or discoverer of truth. The popular image is that science provides the answers to elusive questions and is the key to the world's future. Science on television also tends to deal with basic facts and principles; this helps to reassure us that scientists are certain of the truth about the world, whether it is about DNA or hair follicles.

> 'The nutrients at the base of the hair follicle, the 'goodies', feed the cells and as they grow push up the follicle like toothpaste in a tube.'
>
> *Bodymatters* 21 August 1986

The view of science normally presented on television is a long-standing one. It was first fully formulated by Francis Bacon in the seventeenth century and it has been accepted by most scientists until the twentieth. To put this view crudely, the role of the scientist is systematically to record his findings, accumulate data, and search for general patterns. The scientist verifies these by carrying out further investigations and then shouts *'eureka!'*: another scientific law is discovered. Beyond this law, further hypotheses are formulated to *explain* the known facts; with sufficient 'proof', a new theory is established.

This method of scientific work (known as inductivism) treats statements about observations as if they were sufficient guarantee of the reliability of the laws that flow from them. Most scientists in the past went along with it. It was certainly better than what went before.

The difficulties with this traditional inductivist view are threefold:

- it is based on the logical fallacy that 'proof' is anything other than provisional
- it encourages selective perception
- it ignores the motivation for particular theories

Modern disenchantment with inductivism is based on the realisation that a universal law can be refuted by a single counter-example. Should not scientists, therefore, go all out to try and refute, rather than verify, their theories by observation?

There is also the problem of selective perception. How reliable are our senses? Does even 20/20 vision offer us pure observational data? The more we explore the means of perception, the more we realise that language itself plays a crucial role in formulating what we see. This means our observations are determined by our theories, just as our theories are determined by our observations. We see what we believe as well as believing what we see.

These reservations about inductivism have been put forcefully by Karl Popper and themselves form part of an alternative view of science as a more fallible and provisional process. He sees the scientist's role as more creative. His ideas are not widely known even amongst science educators and are usually encountered on television in philosophy rather than science programmes. (The fact that *Horizon* once made a programme concerned with the illusory objectivity of science says something about how that particular series can sometimes provide exceptions to the general rule.)

Popper starts from the position that what we call knowledge must be provisional. And its pursuit must be a gamble whose outcome we cannot predict at the outset. This is what distinguishes science from belief and from myth. As Thomas Kuhn has pointed out, most facts 'known' at any given time have turned out to seem different or even false when seen from the perspective of new theory. Science proceeds on the back of an unending sequence of stringent attempts to explore the weaknesses of theories. It tries to accelerate the elimination of bad ideas and ensure the survival of the best ones. We then base our technical decisions on the basis of 'the best of our current knowledge'.

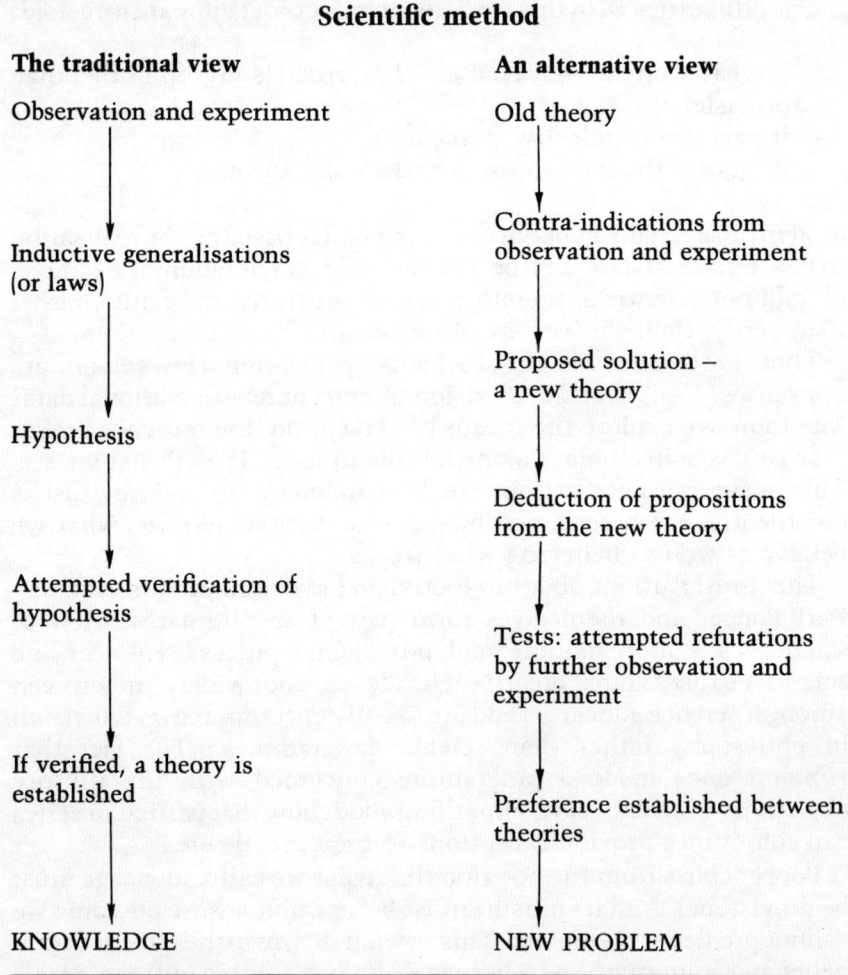

Scientific method

The traditional view

Observation and experiment

↓

Inductive generalisations
(or laws)

↓

Hypothesis

↓

Attempted verification of
hypothesis

↓

If verified, a theory is
established

↓

KNOWLEDGE

An alternative view

Old theory

↓

Contra-indications from
observation and experiment

↓

Proposed solution –
a new theory

↓

Deduction of propositions
from the new theory

↓

Tests: attempted refutations
by further observation and
experiment

↓

Preference established between
theories

↓

NEW PROBLEM

Science is not simply a body of data or knowledge, but a set of theories. It offers a particular way of understanding the world. On one level, science is what scientists do, but it cannot be only that. Neil Ryder suggests that science can be thought of as, 'the attempt by a scientist to persuade other scientists to a particular view about some scientific issues' (Ryder, 1982, p. 70).

Our perception of science also consists of a selection from all that is said and done in its name. It is not so much an objective entity as a form of discourse, like television. And if this is true, it may be more useful to think of television as a parallel (or rival) form of discourse rather than as merely a means of disseminating or distorting science. We are then left with a hybrid discourse which might be called 'telescience' and which is subject to the distinctive rules and conventions of its two parent discourses.

The courage to question

Television rarely presents scientists as putting forward hunches or as self-critical and unsure about their investigations. Nor is science presented as a creative activity in which making 'discoveries' involves intuitive and non-rational forms of thought. Yet most scientists themselves are only too aware that the Popperian view is more in line with the way they actually work. The scientific process is, in reality, much more muddled and uncertain than the way it is packaged by television. Television presents a traditional, mythical view of science and the scientist. But the real world of science tends to work within a Popperian framework.

Producers of television science programmes give themselves the task of presenting something interesting about science. But it is not in their interests to undermine the audience's belief in the scientist and his work, and so the traditional view of science as an inductive process based on facts is fostered, encouraging audiences to believe that scientific knowledge represents absolute truth. If knowledge *were* presented as provisional, programmes would have to be made which were long and difficult with more questions being asked than answers being given.

Rarely are programmes presented on our screens which challenge the traditional view of science; nowhere is science presented as a process which encourages scepticism and humility in the face of an unknown world. Until makers of science programmes have the courage to question the traditional view of science and employ all the techniques available in this quest, we are going to be left with the inevitable dazzling array of gadgets and jokes which soothe away our anxiety about those responsible (amongst other things) for Chernobyl and Germ Warfare establishments. The real question is: do we want to know what scientists are really doing and how they do it? Are we, in fact, prepared to take the risks and face the consequences which such knowledge entails?

3

Serial Science

The fourth *Real World* series began its run on the ITV network on Monday June 3rd 1985 at 7pm. Seven programmes, each dedicated to a different scientific topic, continued through the summer. What did these programmes have in common with each other? How did they relate to other television science programmes? Are there any consistent patterns in the kind of issues dealt with in the series or in similar ones? If so, what criteria are beneath the selection of the particular scientific stories which are featured?

This chapter explores these patterns and examines some of the continuities of style, tone and treatment which are also evident in television science programmes.

Creating a story

'If there is a one-liner, that one-liner is sufficient for me to say there must be a programme in there – no matter what.'

Garfield Kennedy, producer of *The Real World*, obviously has a clear and dramatic view of how his own programmes begin. *Dead as the Dodo?* began from a line in *The Guardian*, 19 November 1984: 'Scientists in U.S. and Britain have succeeded in cloning preserved fragments of genetic material from animals long dead.' He was immediately convinced that this story would capture the audience's attention and once he had been given the 'go-ahead', he set about searching for the scientists who could, as he put it, 'open up a door on the universe'.

Although this may seem somewhat haphazard, the recurrence of certain features in television science programmes suggests that there is an implicit system of rules in operation, which is not apparent to producers or viewers. Identifying these patterns will help us to uncover and examine some of the unwritten rules of science programmes on television.

How does an item of scientific news become a 'story'? In the case of *The Real World*, as with similar programmes, the selection of potential stories effectively begins with the first planning meeting.

> 'At the meeting there were some pretty hairy old chestnuts being thrown around like 'The Weather'. We were always going to do a programme on the weather. Magnetism was another subject, I'm not sure that 'The Technology of Fleet Street' wasn't a subject that was being thrown about. A young, new producer . . . Garfield Kennedy . . . had the crazy idea of doing a programme about the possible ability to recreate extinct animals.'
>
> Michael Rodd, Presenter, *The Real World*

The criteria used by broadcasters are not at all explicit but based on unspoken perceptions of the basic human psychology and of what makes a 'story' worthwhile. In operational terms, this means having a good 'nose' for a story or having a journalist's 'instinctive' awareness of what is worth following up and developing. As Thelma Rumsey, researcher on *The Real World*, said of Garfield Kennedy's idea: 'I wasn't quite sure whether that would stand up for half an hour's programming. But he was very convincing about it, very enthusiastic.'

The evidence that we have from the production of *The Real World* rarely explains precisely why decisions were made. Alec Nisbett of the BBC offers a more analytical perspective:

> There is a bias in the selection of topics towards: substantial recent advances which extend or change the shape of a field of study; changes in direction, for example paradigm shifts; problems affecting the scientific process; observations, insights or discoveries which appear to require substantial public action, expenditure or

changes of attitude; presentations by individuals who can communicate infectious enthusiasm; and visually attractive subjects.

There is a bias against: additional detail, confirming previously reported advances; technical detail which holds up the flow of an argument and thereby impedes the understanding of broad principles; 'talking heads' who could attract labels such as 'worthy', 'academic', or 'slow' or who use too much jargon or talk down; forms of presentation which could be done as well in other media, for example radio; and 'teachy' set ups.   (Nisbett, 1984, p. 16)

If we accept that science programmes share some of the characteristics of news bulletins it is appropriate to use the criteria suggested by Galtung and Ruge to analyse the processes whereby items are selected for inclusion.

Selecting the issues

These criteria were designed originally to apply to news bulletins. They are grouped in two categories. The first deals with general conditions which will apply to all selection processes whilst the second is more applicable to the 'North Western corner of the world' and consists of 'culture-bound' criteria.

General conditions

i) *Frequency.*   If the event has a time-span consistent with the time it takes for a programme to be completed then its chance of selection is high. The announcement of a scientific discovery or the launch of a new gadget falls within the time frame of the programme makers. Trends and gradual changes in scientific thought are not easily focused into a single programme. If such items are to find their way into science programmes then some milestone must have been reached. This allows the programme makers the opportunity of reflection whilst heralding the 'manufactured' short frequency event. Nisbett's phrase 'recent advances' matches Galtung and Ruge's first condition.

ii) *Threshold.*   The size of the event may draw the programme maker's attention. A small step forward in understanding may go unnoticed by the programme makers and press alike, and will never reach the screens. A significant advance – a heart-transplant technique or the discovery of a new comet – will bring the documentary makers from all corners of the world. Nisbett uses the word 'substantial' to highlight the importance of the 'threshold' of an event.

iii) *Unambiguity.*   Events do not have to be simple, but it helps. Very complex scientific ideas will tend to distract from the narrative in a science programme and are therefore generally avoided. Perhaps more important than the simplicity of the idea is its need to be clearly explained. The viewer must at least be given the chance of understanding what is involved in the issue: the event must be unambiguous. Nisbett emphasises the need for clarity by referring to a bias against ideas which contain 'technical detail which holds up the flow of an argument and thereby impedes the understanding of broad principles'.

iv) *Meaningfulness.*   This is perhaps the most important criterion for successfully capturing the attention of the audience. The issue must be seen to impinge on the life of the viewer. Nisbett claims a bias for items which 'appear to require substantial public action, expenditure or changes of attitude'. Recent advances in technology which may ultimately affect the lifestyle of the manual labourer are likely to rank more highly in the programme makers' agenda than advances in rice horticultural practice, for instance.

Issues which are not central to the viewer *may* take shape if they ultimately affect the home culture. A rice-growing revolution will, for instance, have economic implications for the home cereal exporters. The programme maker will then have to find an 'angle' which increases the meaningfulness of the issue for the audience. Silverstone's account of the making of the *Horizon* programme on rice horticulture in the Far East (*A New Green Revolution?*) graphically illustrates the producer's struggle to find an angle which would make the programme relevant to a British audience. The science was novel and intrinsically interesting to the specialist viewer but of little interest to the general viewer. The angle which enhanced the programme's meaningfulness for the home audience was the issue of British grant-aid to developing countries and the impact of economic development in countries to which we export substantial quantities of home grown cereal.

v) *Consonance.*   Galtung and Ruge developed this criterion for the selection of an item in a news bulletin whose occurrence is based on current expectations. As the public awareness of the likelihood of violence at football matches has grown in the 1980s so has the news coverage of that violence. Even at relatively trouble-free games the few instances of violence, both off and on the field, are widely reported in the media. A minor incident which would have gone unreported a decade ago can become front page news. The producers of science documentaries do not generally have the same powers as the news journalist. They cannot 'wish' a discovery into being. They can, however, pre-empt public concern over scientific issues by presenting them in a way which confirms existing expectations.

vi) *Unexpectedness.*   Scientific advances and discoveries are by their very nature unpredictable. The scientific community may struggle for years to perfect a cure for cancer. The mundane battle through the years is rarely of interest to the programme maker. The 'frequency' of the event also compounds the bias against such programmes. Sudden, unexpected breakthroughs are another matter.

Novelty attracts the attention of the curious audience. The BBC's *Tomorrow's World* series relies almost exclusively on the novelty aspect of its gadgets to attract its audience. The 'Gee-whiz!' approach to science programme making is one of the most effective popular science programme formats. The ability of the medium to show rare discoveries to wide audiences is highlighted by Nisbett who favours 'visually attractive' subjects and shuns items which may 'be done as well in other media, for example, radio'. If the item is visually attractive, it will score highly on any producer's list of items for inclusion.

'Visually attractive' can mean many different things. In science programmes this may range from spectacular scenery to spectacular technology. Film of animals in their natural habitat must rank highly in series like the BBC's *Life on Earth* and *The Natural World*.

vii) *Continuity.*   If an item has been covered once by a programme maker then it is unlikely that further developments in that field will become the focus of future programmes. The subject may become a 'running story', and a favourite issue for the producer. If the item has received extensive coverage on a rival station its chances of developing into a programme become remote.

viii) *Composition.*   A mixture of different scientific topics will be covered in a season's run of a documentary series like *Horizon* or *The Real World*. The series editor or executive producer will be conscious of the need to balance the output. In this way, relatively low priority items may reach production. Within a single science magazine programme like *Tomorrow's World* there will be a balancing act in each weekly episode. In a single science documentary there will be a number of items competing for inclusion which never reach the final programme because of the need to balance the composition. This applies in the same way to a whole series of *The Real World*.

Culture-bound conditions

Galtung and Ruge also developed criteria for the selection of news items on the basis of their pertinence to developed, Western societies rather than to other parts of the world. These culture-bound criteria for selection include references to 'élite' nations (mostly the developed countries) and 'élite' persons (well-known personalities).

Many scientific advances are made in 'élite nations' in the developed world, so it is obvious that those countries will dominate discussions of science. The selection of stories is here dictated more by the economics of science than by the familiarity or unfamiliarity of other cultures.

All scientists may be considered 'élite' persons in the broadest application of this criterion. They command respect and even reverence in the minds of many members of society. In a narrower application of the criterion, however, élite persons are few and far between in the world of science. Nobel prize-winners each have their moment of glory but the tedium of research finds them fading from the public eye. Notable exceptions are to be found more in the past than in the present. Einstein and Darwin rank highly in public awareness. Élite persons are usually to be found affected by science rather than affecting scientific change. Film stars with AIDS, for instance, focus the public attention on issues which might otherwise pass unnoticed.

Presenters of scientific programmes may take on the role of scientists and as such may become 'élite persons'. Occasionally they are scientists who make the transition to television and make their name because of it. Few people have any knowledge of the scientific work of David Bellamy or Magnus Pike before they became television science presenters. Other presenters find their way from the dramatic arts, the law or journalism into the role of surrogate scientists, e.g. Michael Rodd and Peter McCann of *Tomorrow's World*.

Personalisation is also an important criterion for selection. An audience relates more easily to the work of specific scientists than to the work of a research institution or university. Thus, there is a tendency towards 'presentations by individuals who can communicate infectious enthusiasm'. If a programme maker finds a story but is unable to locate a scientist who has charisma and the ability to express the issues clearly and with energy, then either the story will fall or a presenter will have to carry the issue to the audience.

The final criterion for the selection of an issue is *negativity*. In news terms 'bad news is good news'. In the context of a news bulletin bad news meets most of Galtung and Ruge's criteria: it is unexpected, unambiguous, it happens quickly, and is consonant with general expectations about the state of the world and hence its threshold is lower than that for positive news.

In science programmes, however, this criterion is, significantly, the one most strenuously rejected. As the whole mythology of science rests on the notion of the advancement of mankind, it would be counter-productive to stress the all too frequent failures in scientific research. By its very nature, research often poses more questions than it solves. But to make science programmes about failures to understand the world in which we live would risk disappointing the majority of the audience. Such is the way that television science finds itself bound to sustain the traditional mythology of scientific endeavour.

The Real World 1985

With Galtung and Ruge's criteria in mind, it is worth looking more closely at the individual programmes in the 1985 series of *The Real World*. It is immediately noticeable that the stories concentrate on the successes of science.

The topics included in the series are diverse and show no obvious links with each other. What holds them together, however, is a common format and style, clearly exemplified in the *Dodo* programme. They all link interviews and pieces of film shot around the world with studio comment and explanation. In some there is a participat-

POPULAR SCIENCE PROGRAMMES

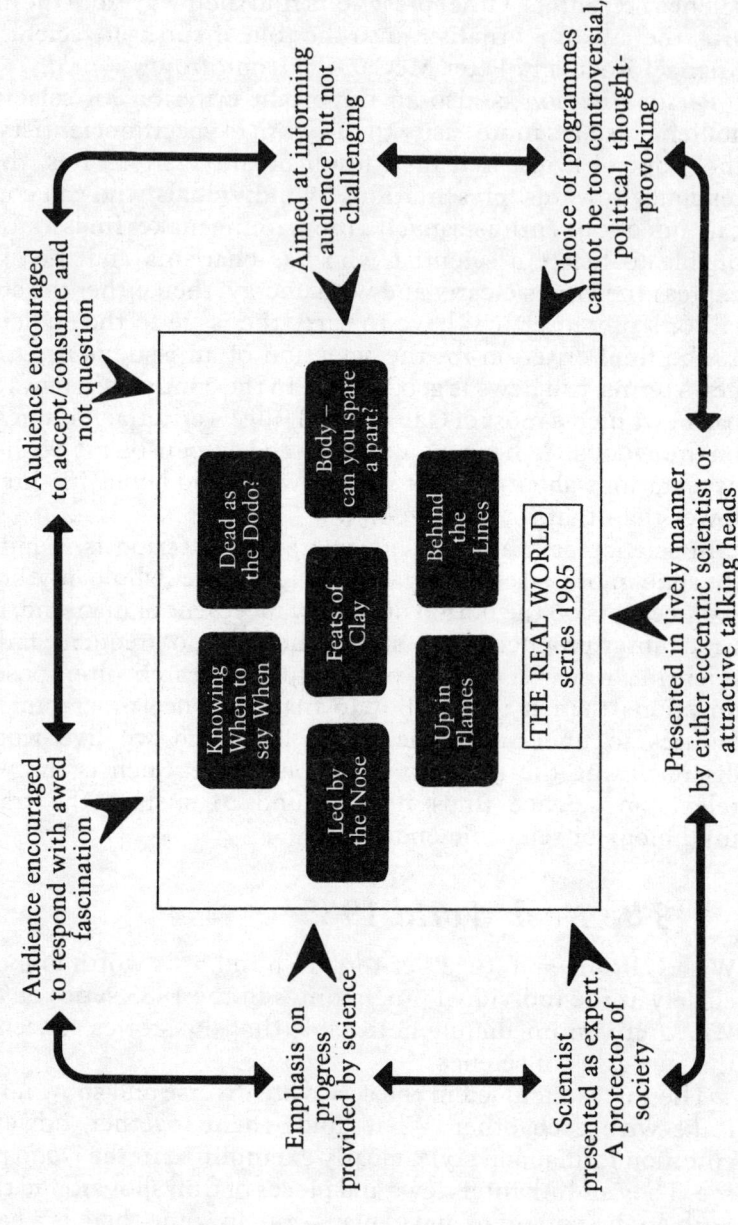

Aimed at informing audience but not challenging

Audience encouraged to accept/consume and not question

Choice of programmes cannot be too controversial, political, thought-provoking

Audience encouraged to respond with awed fascination

Dead as the Dodo?

Body – can you spare a part?

Knowing When to say When

Feats of Clay

Behind the Lines

Led by the Nose

Up in Flames

THE REAL WORLD series 1985

Presented in lively manner by either eccentric scientist or attractive talking heads

Emphasis on progress provided by science

Scientist presented as expert. A protector of society

ing audience, in others the two series presenters and invited guest speakers are the only people in the studio.

Each programme, of course, begins with the same short computer-generated title-sequence. We are then invited to stay and watch by a mini-trailer, which may pose a question or hint at a scandal. In most cases, the best images used in the programme are offered in a 'sneak preview'. Once intrigued by the opening, we see the programme title and launch into the narrative.

Space does not allow for a full analysis of each programme here, but a look at *Dead as the Dodo*'s fellow-programmes highlights some of the themes and ideologies embodied in them. It also gives us a broader focus on the way science is represented in the series.

The studio set features a collection of giant multi-coloured mock crystals towering like spires behind the presenters. It remains the same throughout the series, but the largely uncluttered studio is also specifically set for each programme with artifacts related to the subject in focus. In *Dead as the Dodo?* we see the studio floor used for a genealogical tree. In *Feats of Clay*, the studio is adorned with examples of the latest advances in materials technology, including a Lotus car. This set-design bears similarities to other poular science programmes, in particular the design now well-established in the BBC's *Tomorrow's World*. The audience is expected to recognise these symbolic representations of scientific and technological endeavour.

Feats of Clay takes us into the future of materials technology. By special reference to the motor car we are given a preview of the advances being made in the materials used in manufacturing industry. We are promised everlasting bodywork and super-efficient engines in the car of the future. The programme predicts the ultimate demise of metals, to be replaced by composites and ceramics.

In some ways the series can be compared to a tabloid newspaper. It is a popular science series which assumes an audience with little knowledge of the issues discussed. Like all popular media, it uses everday language and avoids technical words and phrases or scientific jargon. In *Dead as the Dodo?* this is acknowledged explicitly when, in the final piece to camera, Michael Rodd comments 'Now, if any of you find all this a little complicated . . .'

The series is also overtly patriotic. In several programmes claims are made specifically on behalf of British advances in technology (e.g. in *Knowing When to Say When*, *Up in Flames* and *Behind the Lines*).

Up in Flames is a particularly spectacular programme. The programme makers had managed to acquire 'exclusive access to historic footage' of a plane crash. But the programme focuses on the controlled testing of a fire-reducing Anti-Misting Kerosene developed by ICI in Britain. The product was not a success but the programme tries to salvage its reputation (and that of science?) by explaining the unexpectedly adverse conditions during the 'crash'. The narrative is woven around film recorded during a Controlled Impact Demonstration (CID), in which a passenger aircraft was deliberately crashed at Edwards Air Force Base in California. It centres on the political and economic consequences of the test failure. The availability of moving pictures, taken from many angles during the CID, seems to have been the main reason for the programme being made. The programme also offers a good illustration of Galtung and Ruge's criteria of 'unexpectedness' and 'meaningfulness'.

Behind the Lines is, in fact, a look forward to developments in television technology. Two rival systems are doing battle for the future market in domestic televisions. The Japanese, with the support of the Americans, are developing a 'High Definition Television' (HDTV) which is heralded as a giant step forward in picture quality. But this new system implies that all existing television hardware would become obsolete, and the cost of re-equipping would be astronomic. The European system, on the other hand, would maintain the current 625-line hardware. The battle lines are drawn in a struggle in which the consumer has no say. We are invited to see it as a contest between the home-grown product and the manufacturing power of Japan (with prototypes of their new technology ready and waiting for a worldwide standard to be agreed). *Knowing When to Say When* considers the related but somewhat opposed topics of conception and contraception. The idea for the programme came from recent scientific advances in D-I-Y diagnostic testing of ovulation. As a major breakthrough both in contraception and as an aid to fertility, the topic has broad appeal. The bonus of having access in the studio to two rival systems as an 'exclusive' adds prestige to the programme.

Where the programme differs somewhat from the familiar format is in its constant referral to a Roman Catholic priest in the audience who passes ecclesiastical judgement on the new techniques of contraception, and to an Indian doctor (in national costume) who comments on the relevance of the new technology to the Third

World. We should note the brief contribution of this scientist, Dr Primilla Senanayake, Medical Director of the International Planned Parenthood Federation. She is the only female scientist to make a contribution in front of camera in the whole series. We do see women in the audience for some of the other programmes. But they are asked only to make relatively trivial judgements on odours, television picture quality and the simplicity of home pregnancy tests. In the studio the presenters reflect this male-dominated society. As Garfield Kennedy comments, 'Michael Rodd does, and Sue Jay says'.

Led by the Nose was heralded as a television first. 'Aromavision' had arrived. The theme for this programme is the human sense of smell and it was to be the largest test of this sense ever staged. The programme was supported by 'scratch cards' which had been previously circulated with the *TV Times*. Numbered panels on the cards were to be scratched at an appropriate signal during the programme. Once scratched, the panel gave off an odour and the audience (in the studio and at home) were invited to identify the aroma.

Body—Can You Spare a Part? is a significant departure from the series' usual concerns. Its main emphasis is on the ethical questions raised by advances in transplant surgery. The programme opens with an American discussing the cost of providing a kidney for transplant. We are assured that the cost of $12,300 is not for the kidney, but to cover the expense of removing and transporting it. Throughout the programme we are invited to consider the finances of transplant surgery and the ethics of selling human organs. Nowhere else in the series is the audience asked to make value judgements of the kind raised in this programme.

Explaining things

Michael Rodd describes *The Real World* as 'a programme about science but not of interest exclusively to scientists'. In order to be of interest to a wide audience the series aims to 'deformalise the subject matter – avoiding buzzwords and acknowledging that certain subjects are complicated and require thinking about'. How effective have the programme makers been in presenting the subject-matter of *Dead as the Dodo?*

'It zips along, and that is on account of the amount of information we try to put in', says Michael Rodd. There is no doubt that this programme is full of 'science'. The subjects range from biology and geology through to astronomy and archaeology. There will be a few viewers who bring to the programme such a range of specific background knowledge to allow them to make sense of all the concepts involved. Some viewers will already have come across some of the material, but the majority will know nothing of the science included in the programme.

A vital link in the story depends on an understanding of the cloning of DNA. The explanation of what DNA does is given whilst looking at a test-tube containing a colourless, viscous liquid which is described as being 'sticky'. Are we to believe that this 'sticky' liquid is the 'foundation of life itself'? In a later explanation, the amino acid sequence in the DNA of a quagga is compared to that of a modern zebra's DNA. How the 'sticky' liquid turns into a string of letters is not elaborated. Those in the know will need no further explanation to see the relevance of the sequence similarity. Will the vast majority of the audience be left confused?

What are we told about cloning? The explanation is long in coming and brief when it comes. Cloning consists of DNA being copied in the laboratory, over and over again, for research and investigation. The programme speculates upon and even draws its title from the possibility of cloning fully developed animals from ancient tissue samples. Eminent scientists are asked to join in the fun by speculating on future developments of the technique. Is this all we are to learn about cloning?

As with the other programmes in the series, this programme is supported by a four-page glossy A4 leaflet. Together with some information contained in the programme, it provides background scientific knowledge, photographs and diagrams. The language used in the 'back-up' material is much more technical than that used in the programme. It is clearly aimed at a specific section of the overall audience. The main category of viewer who wrote in to TVS for the 'back-up' material consisted of teachers. Whereas the programme strives, with varying degrees of success, to entertain as well as to educate, the 'back-up' material eschews entertainment, believing it has already captured the audience. It pulls no punches when it declares, 'It is extremely unlikely that we will ever be able to recreate a living dinosaur, at least not from fossilised remains'.

The 'back-up' material contains a useful glossary to explain those terms taken for granted in the programme, together with a reading list

DNA: Deoxy-Ribonucleic Acid. A carbon based (organic) chemical consisting of a "backbone" of repeating units, alternatively ribose sugar and phosphate, upon which nucleotide bases (the information coding parts) are attached. The whole is paired to an opposite strand (by bonding between complimentary nucleotide bases) and form a double helix.

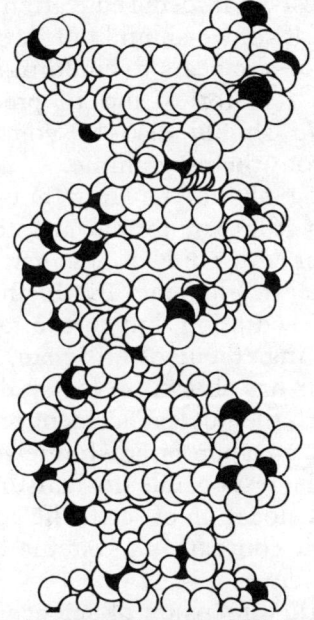

Molecular structure of DNA

'Is that clear?'

for those who wish to delve deeper into the subject. But it also contains some rather surprising (and somewhat morbid) stills of deformed children. The relevance of these is not made clear but, in a curious way, they echo some of the more disturbing aspects of the programme.

What is missing?

Len Masterman suggests that media education involves 'the study of structured absences'. If so, we should not be solely concerned with the way *The Real World* appears to conform so readily to standard criteria in selecting its stories and to predictable formulae in presenting them. We should also be concerned with what is habitually missing from the programme.

Whilst complaining about the growth of interest shown by television science in 'the paranormal and the downright bogus', Bernard Dixon (former editor of *New Scientist*) maintains that what is missing is 'the didactic element'. By this he is not referring to a particular style of presentation, but to the representation of argument, 'the essential ingredient of criticism, the weighing of evidence'. As Neil Ryder has shown, in his study of how the *Nine o' Clock News* dealt with the nuclear accident on Three Mile Island, it is often the lack of an appropriate framework for dealing with information which is responsible for misunderstanding or non-understanding. The dislocation of scientific activity from its social, political and economic contexts is a systematic and serious absence in most television science.

It is the problematic dimension of science which often remains unreported – the clash of ideologies between science as promise and science as threat. Is science the solution to man's problems by producing remedies to his social ills? Or is science the agent which serves to produce produce social and environmental problems? And what strategies will science programme makers employ to make meaning within this ambivalent image of science?

The majority of the science programmes shown by both the BBC and the IBA consider only one side of the relationship between science and society. They proclaim the changes which science will bring to society. But the breathless form of presentation conveys a sense of inevitability, and precludes discussion concerning social choice. As Gardner and Young explain, 'The means of production, the setting of research and development agendas, and the social relations of production and application of scientific knowledge all embody particular positions about the development of society, yet these are rarely examined.' The current modes of science presentation leave many social and political questions unaired. In this way, programme makers are maintaining the tension which exists between science and society: science is seen as one thing, context another.

The notion of the autonomy of knowledge is often uncritically propagated by television, and programme makers defend the boundary between the academy and the market place. But this division is not familiar to scientists at work. In fact, research councils and private foundations are themselves increasingly calling for research which meets the needs of industry. All too often, commercial criteria dictate what research scientists carry out. Television sometimes seems to be performing a public relations exercise on behalf of the scientific community to protect an outdated notion of 'pure' science led by independent research.

As the activities of science and technology increasingly challenge the *status quo*, so television can lead the debate on the social consequences of these changes. Television has an important role to play in the critical evaluation of the issues raised by science rather than in protecting a privileged position for it.

PRESENTATION

How are scientific issues presented?

In this section, our focus moves from how scientific ideas are represented onto how they are presented on screen. This means concentrating on the surface features of the programme or 'text' in some detail. But we should remember that the distinctions between presentation and representation are merely a convenience for us and that the concepts are in reality inseparable from each other. This section looks first of all at the process of production in order to establish how the criteria discussed in the first section of the book operate in relation to the development of a particular programme. We can then go on to discuss the stylistic and narrative features of the finished programme.

At the simplest level, this means examining the particular sounds and images which make the programme what it is. The title-sequence provides a convenient way of investigating how the visual aspects of presentation (picture composition, framing, lighting, graphics, captions, photographs, props, lighting and special effects) interact with the acoustic aspects (music, voice-over, synch. sound and special effects). We can also examine the cutting between shots and the editing of longer sequences to see how they create an overall rhythm for the programme. This is illustrated by the way in which the different interviewees are integrated into the programme. The style and tone of the programme involve more subtle aspects of presentation which are explored here by an analysis of the language used by presenters and interviewees.

Most important, however, is the way the various strands of the programme are woven together into a continuous whole of 26 minutes' duration. Garfield Kennedy draws attention to how the programme should be 'choppy and bumpy and almost uncomfortable' through bringing in constant shifts of attention or 'gosh! factors'. We also examine the way items are consistently compressed into limited programme space and fine-tuned into a smooth and seamless 'flow'.

Finally, we examine how the programme's narrative takes the form of a detective story by leading us through various 'clues'. This narrative has two inseparable aspects: story and argument. The story is concerned with the 'what next?' aspects of the narrative, while the argument is concerned with its 'why?' and 'how?'. Both, of course, are essential if the programme is to achieve both interest and understanding.

4

Producing a Programme

The phases of production
Research; Filming; Studio recording; Editing and approval;
Transmission

When the credits roll at the end of *Dead as the Dodo?*, twenty-six
names are listed, each with a specific role in the production team; and
more than one hundred people were involved in some way with the
making of the programme. Programme making is essentially an
interactive process. No two programme teams work in the same way
and even within a series the method of working off-screen can vary
from programme to programme as much as the style of presentation
on-screen. All kinds of factors play a part in this: the demands of the
subject matter, levels of staffing, constraints of time and finance and,
ultimately, the working relationship within the team itself. This
chapter looks at how these various factors interact to produce a
particular kind of programme.

The phases of production

We are not concerned here with the origins of the *Real World* series in
1982, nor with how it developed in the following years. It would
certainly be interesting to look back at Michael Blackstad's original
proposals for the series and how he 'sold' the idea of an answer to
Tomorrow's World to his colleagues in the newly enfranchised
company. It would also be interesting to unearth the process whereby
what was originally a regional programme managed to find a slot in
the network schedules.

But we are focusing here on the production of a single programme
within a particular series of *The Real World*. This involves looking

briefly at the initial discussions about the idea for the programme and then following through the development of that idea into what was actually transmitted. This also enables us to describe the roles of many of the programme team, even though we can only follow through a fraction of the planning and development process.

The problem of how to simplify and arrange the different elements in the story so that they would present a coherent narrative does not figure in the surviving documents. We should not therefore assume from the absence of documentary evidence that there was little attention paid to this aspect of presentation. The producer's concern with constructing a comprehensible argument is in the end a very personal and even private activity. What is clear is that items, once recorded, became relatively fixed. The running order could be (and was) changed, but the items remained more or less the same. The argument was limited by the availability of material and by the producer's skill in shaping it into a coherent form. In the event, a great deal of attention was given to other aspects of presentation like the studio sequences, and we can see how this affected the finished programme.

The whole production process can be seen in terms of distinct phases, each of which compresses a large amount of work into a smaller space for the next phase of production. In reality, of course, the process is much more complex than such an abstract model implies. Each phase contains a multiplicity of different elements and there is overlap between them. Individuals from the production team are involved in various ways during the different phases of production, and they

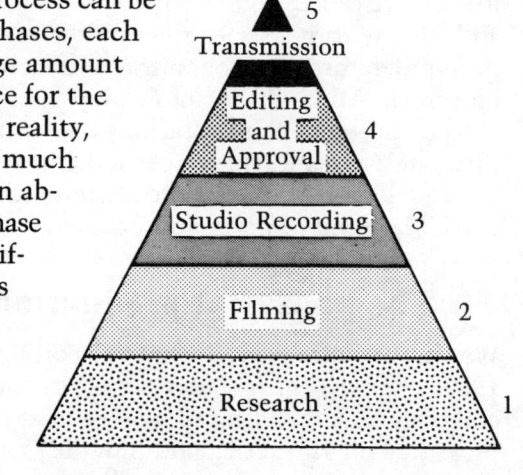

are working on up to seven programmes at a time for a single series. Nor is each phase absolutely distinct. Editing, for example, takes place both after filming and after the studio recording. In a more general sense, too, the process of selection and compression begins at the very first programme ideas meeting.

The production of a single programme

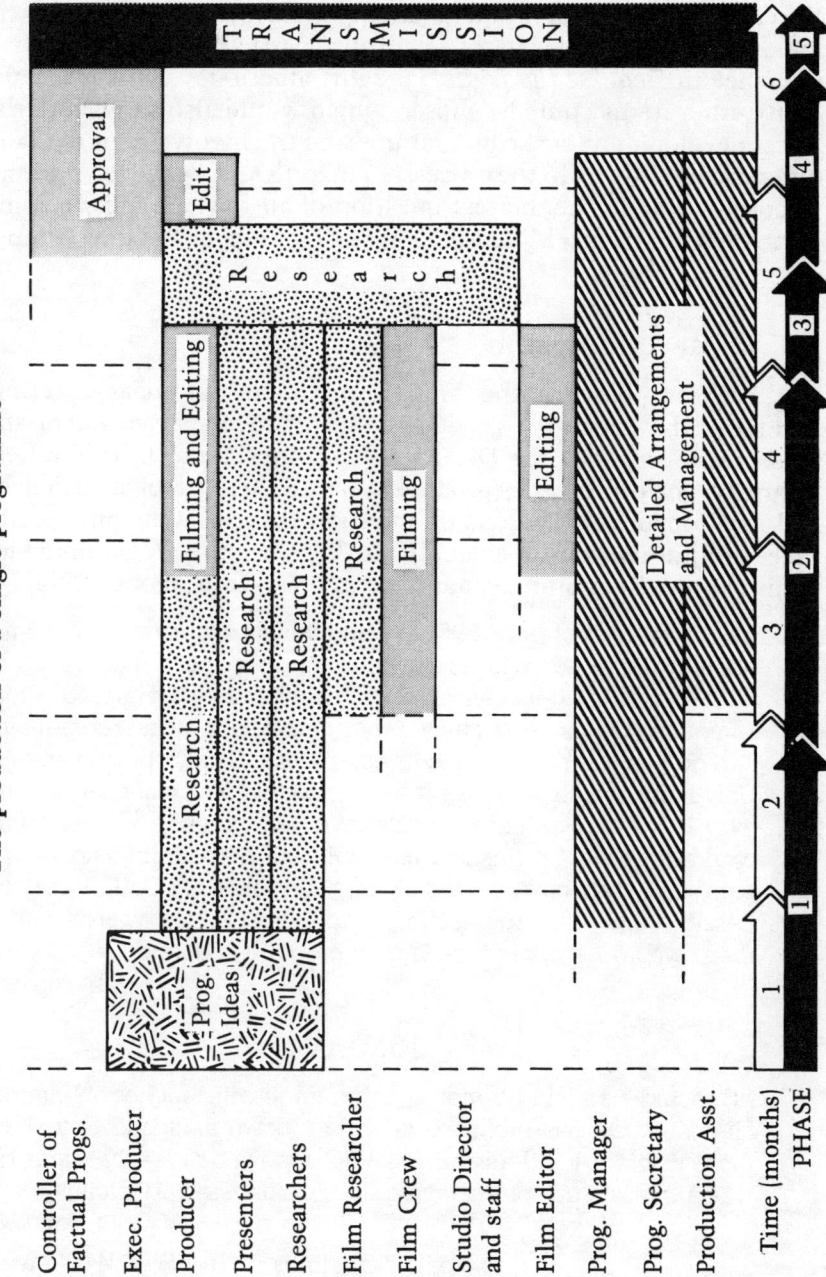

We can achieve a clearer understanding of the production process by looking beyond this general level at a particular and distinctive sequence in *Dead as the Dodo?*: the introduction of Ramapithecus. Many other items could be chosen which would also show both the linear development of the programme and the involvement of many different individuals in the process. Ramapithecus, however, plays an important part in the 'biggest question of all – where did we come from?' which Michael Rodd asks at the opening of the programme.

Phase 1: Research

The earliest phase of the process is the initial ideas meeting, involving the executive producer, the producers, researchers and presenters. The idea for *Dead as the Dodo?* came from Garfield Kennedy, one of the series producers, on the strength of an article he had read (opposite). There is no mention there of Ramapithecus or indeed of human genealogy at all. At this stage the programme idea focused on extinct animals and recent discoveries about DNA.

> It is possible to create life from living things, culture cells, but what about using dead cells? Is sperm in a frozen sperm-bank dead or alive? To what extent can you recreate life from what is dead? From something that is dead, can you work out what it is and recreate it – and do you *want* to recreate it? Scientists at San Diego Zoo and the University of California are researching this. The last quagga died over 100 years ago and scientists have taken a piece of the skin and worked out what it was and how different it was from a horse or a zebra and they have started cloning sequences of DNA. It may be possible that, if a large section of an extinct animal was available, there would be enough cells to work out a sequence.
>
> 21 Jan 1985

> QUAGGA

> [it] should be a mind-bending programme with touches of Hammer films in it. GK has promised to write it down in simple English for those who don't understand – like PG. One good idea that came out was a chessboard of the studio floor demonstrating evolution.
>
> 11 Feb 1985
>
> Notes on meetings of *The Real World* team

Quagga gets ready to gallop again

By Anthony Tucker, Science Correspondent

The dodo may not be quite dead, the great mammoth might be stirring, and a zebra-like horse, the quagga – which became extinct just over a century ago, when the last one died in Amsterdam Zoo – is still here.

Scientists in the US and Britain have succeeded in cloning preserved fragments of genetic material from preserved fragments of animals long dead.

It turns out that under the right conditions the genetic blueprint DNA is as tough as old boots.

In the latest investigation, scientists from the University of California at Berkeley and the San Diego Zoo have managed to isolate and examine in great detail the DNA from a fragment of quagga muscle that had been preserved in a museum.

The quagga, related to the mountain zebra and to the horse – and much farther back in evolution to the cow – would be expected to have genetic material whose chemical sequence relates closely to these species.

Given that the structure of human haemoglobin differs from that of the horse by only a couple of minor molecular shifts, the genetic material of quagga and horse would be expected to be very similar.

According to a report in *Nature*, this is exactly what has been found.

Working on the cloning of short sections of genetic material taken from tissue cell components known as mitochondria, the Californian group has stitched together long clonable sections whose minor differences from horse DNA could well be merely expressing the species difference.

Although living relatives of the mammoth are less easy to find, the confirmation that quagga genetic material has survived so well in its dried crystalline form lends reassuring support to work in Britain.

Leicester University's department of genetics is piecing together and cloning DNA from the frozen remains of extinct mammoths.

If, instead of mitochondrial DNA, genetic material from a cell nucleus could be cloned, recovering the genetic blueprint for the complete animal could be the next step.

Soon, it will be possible to slip exotic genetic material into a viable egg and produce a surviving hybrid.

The quagga-zebra and the quagga-horse might put evolution into reverse, and another 100 years could see the quagga back in Amsterdam.

The Guardian – Monday 19/11/1984

Once the initial idea had aroused sufficient interest to merit further research, the producer and researchers followed up the direct and indirect leads given in the article by reading other accounts of similar work, contacting the scientists working in this area and gathering together details of their research.

Up until this point, Ramapithecus had no bearing on the programme except as an integral part of the research of Dr Jerold Lowenstein, who was selected as a likely interviewee. Lowenstein's comparative work on Ramapithecene proteins and human and ape proteins had established that in fact Ramapithecus was not man's nearest ancestor, but an ape. Initially, there had been one thread of interest running through the programme research: the cloning of extinct creatures. Now there was a second: the implications of work on proteins for the story of human evolution.

The producer and researcher visited Dr Lowenstein for a preliminary meeting in California a week before the film crew arrived. The interview which was actually filmed began with a question about the significance of Ramapithecus (see transcript in Appendix A).

The task of co-ordinating the decisions and acting upon them belongs to the researcher and producer. The producer's ultimate accountability for the finished programme is fairly common knowledge. The researchers, however, also have significant responsibilities. They are expected to

- suggest programme ideas
- investigate and develop ideas through published sources and personal contacts
- select suitable programme participants
- help define and refine the story
- ensure factual accuracy
- provide necessary props and exhibits

'The initial contact is by phone. You find out whether the people are exciting, interesting to talk to, whether their work is worth following up. A lot of people get cancelled at that point when you say 'that's not what I want'.

You get down to about five or six people that you really need to go and see. You go and see them and talk through their project for three hours, or something like that'.

Thelma Rumsey, Researcher, *The Real World*

Researcher's Notes

TVS – British Museum 19 April 1985

As these ideas are quite complex, I want to put a number of 'props' in the studio to illustrate various points.

TVS Memo 29 April 1985

Thelma is trying to find a stuffed gorilla.

TVS – British Museum 20 May 1985

Teeth to be transported in a secure fashion.

As you will realise, stuffed quaggas do not ever come onto the market.

Royal Scottish Museum – TVS 24 April 1985

I will caution you that our specimen is somewhat faded and by no means pristine.

He had a bad experience with the BBC and will allow no-one else in.

We insist that the specimen is locked in a space to which cleaners . . . have no access.

Supermouse notes

Brinster has the mice but on no account will allow any filming.

The American press have
gone mad over the quagga
and the possibility of
making dinosaurs . . .
as the ultimate defence
against the Russians.

Georgina Mace
(London Zoo)

With genetic
engineering some things
might become possible.

Professor Allan Wilson conversation
30 January 1985

Wilson refuses to appear on TV . . . they've
been inundated with calls from people who've
asked them to take cells from their sons and
keep them to bring their son back to life when
they have the technique refined.

Convince Wilson we're
OK.

Jeffreys conversation (Leicester University)
8 March 1985

He would be happy to talk — but at the moment he
is bound hand and foot.

The discovery is not
that exciting

Olly Ryder

Important to save DNA.
Wishes he knew what he
was saving it for.

IS THE STORY THE NEW
EVOLUTION OF MAN?

Phase 2: Filming

The material filmed on location for *The Real World* largely
determines the final shape of the programme. After the film crew has
returned, the film editor works with the producer in the cutting room
to select the parts of the interviews relevant to the programme. In the
case of *Dead as the Dodo?*, only a short section of the Lowenstein
interview remained in the finished programme but Lowenstein's
research was to provide the basis for a unique entertainment – the
studio-based sequence starring Ramapithecus. However, even at this
stage, Ramapithecus does not appear explicitly in the outline of the
programme that was developing.

QUAGGA PROGRAMME ORDER

1. TITLES

2. STUDIO   around the studio there are pictures of
                      lots of animals (Tasmanian wolf,
                      Steller's sea cow, Mao, Dodo, Quagga,
                      etc). All these animals share one thing

in common – they are extinct. They became extinct either from natural causes or because of man's carelessness.

In the next X years another Y species may be lost.

Animal stuffed in studio – this was last Dodo/Quagga ??? on earth. It died Z hundred years ago. Can we bring them back to life?

3.	TITLES	<u>A GLIMPSE OF IMMORTALITY</u>
4.	FILM	Lowenstein (U. of San Francisco) and the Tasmanian wolf story. Last one died in 1930. Its evolutionary history was disputed but now Lowenstein has solved the species relatedness.
5.	STUDIO	Tasmanian wolf. Evolutionary trees on the floor of the studio – how they have changed since Lowenstein's work.
6.	FILM	San Diego Zoo. Pieces of Quagga and Olly Ryder talking.

Higuchi – talking about Quagga work – how they found out about its evolution by looking at mitochondrial DNA.

How they're going to look at the mammoth, and hopefully insects from 23 million years ago.

Michael Rodd – looking at / touching resin coming out of a tree and insect stuck in resin. Way in which nature preserves.

7.	STUDIO/FILM	Amberised insects from 23 million years ago.
8.	FILM	Lowenstein – how he had looked at fossil man and how work on the DNA of fossil man

and present day man and his relatives have given us a better idea of man's evolution.

9. STUDIO   2 evolutionary trees of humans — one from palaeontologists, one from molecular biologists.

Michael Rodd and chimp — 'I am only 1% different from this chimp.'

Sue with 2 birds that look the same — 'In the same way that this bird is 1% different from this one.'

10. FILM   Most extraordinary story of all. This
     (LIBRARY)   year in Florida Dr. Hauswirth has uncovered 2 human skulls dated at 8000 years old and inside these skulls were intact brains.

Dr. Hauswirth interview ????

11. FILM SAN   San Diego Zoo is preserving DNA of
     DIEGO ZOO   animals so that they will have a library of species which would have helped us in our search nowadays if our ancestors had had the technology.

Interview Olly Ryder.

12. FILM   Supermouse — but what use is the DNA? Well, you can tamper with it and insert bits of genetic material.

Transtime California — so perhaps we shouldn't be freezing complete humans but preserving them like this?

13. STUDIO   Row of test tubes with DNA in. 'This is Michael Rodd reduced to basics' — scoop out some of DNA.

14. END CREDITS   Over track over test tubes and something suitable in V. O.

Phase 3: Studio recording

One problem that emerged was how to present Lowenstein's complex discoveries in a way that was immediately comprehensible and strong in visual impact. The first plan – which quickly foundered – was to have a full-sized Ramapithecus model in the studio. No such model could be located. Stuffed orang-utans, gorillas and chimpanzees could all be hired but there seemed to be only two ways of representing Ramapithecus – by using the teeth and jawbones available from the Natural History Museum, or by using a picture. Neither was a satisfactory alternative. The reconstruction of man's evolutionary tree required the palpable presence of Ramapithecus. Garfield Kennedy, the producer, made the decision to use an actor in costume.

Bob Franklin, the studio director, had already been thinking about how to realise the programme's ideas visually and spatially. He was quite clear what sort of programme it would be:

> *Quaggas*: – basically, the theme of this programme can be found in *Frankenstein*. It's full of creepy stuff about bringing extinct species back from the dead. We will be tracing some family trees (animal and human) and it might be fun to use the crane and do this with models on a specially designed floor. The studio will probably be full of stuffed animals, blow-ups, skulls, bones (and a real live chimpanzee).

The researcher's list of necessary props for the studio gives a glimpse of the variety of elements to be included:

Dead as the Dodo?: props list

1 Stuffed orang-utan/chimpanzee/gorilla (all self-supporting)
  NB Cancel gibbon

2 Cardboard quagga (life size)
  Need colour picture to post to D. Tasker

3 Dinosaur diorama – phone Fred Triccas – how's it going?

4 Dinosaur bones and vertebrae

5 Cut away bone to show inside

6   6 – 8 test tubes containing DNA – need good clean ones.
Test tube rack (adapt one used in *Babies*)
Something to twist DNA strands on

7   Various stills – 2 line drawings – mammoth
3 dinosaur pics – ask D. Tasker where they are

8   Ramapithecus made-up man

9   Ramapithecus teeth and jaw from Turkey – when discovered

10   Meteorite (for hand-held)

11   Piece of amber containing insects

12   Fred Hoyle's book

A much fuller picture of how the elements were co-ordinated, however, can be gained from the preliminary thinking of the studio director. His task was to see that the elements make sense in relation to each other and to the conception of the programme as a whole. The set needed to be flexible and allow the presenters to move around freely and naturally within it. This had to be done within the constraints of a style common to the whole series. His notes to the designer let us into the picture:

Basic set

Presentation to camera will be much in the same mould: singles or two-handers, sometimes standing, sometimes sitting, sometimes on the move. No desk. The basic set needs to be simple and flexible, easily trucked to provide clean, elegant, unfussy foreground and background interest to shots composed over the full range from single MCU to full-length two-shot, static or on the move from point to point. It should also allow for seated interviews with 'expert' participants, singly or possibly in pairs.

Now, some specifics

Bear in mind that this programme has no participating group beyond the odd expert or two; so we won't need an area for group chat. We want to have a stuffed quagga (size of a zebra) in the studio

(Garfield knows where he can lay his hands on one – Edinburgh, I suspect). I think he's also negotiating for a dinosaur. There will, as I mentioned before, be skulls and bones and maybe a skeleton for display. But the two major set elements over and above the basic set are as follows:

(i) two family trees (painted? taped?) on the floor which I can shoot either from a crane or a tower. I enclose a diagram which is approximately right but exact details will follow. I don't think that the trees themselves are all that complicated but what interests me is what happens at the ends of the branches – you will note that they end at human/chimp/gorilla/orang/gibbon. How can we achieve this? Actual stuffed animals? Blow-ups? Think about it.

(ii) Garfield would like to do something on how the continents actually split apart from the original single land-mass (which I think was called Gondwanaland) millions of years ago. One solution is rostrum film but he and I like the idea of a kind of large jigsaw on the floor (shot from above) which is pulled apart (we could find you the diagrams which show how they all fitted together).

Bob Franklin, Studio Director,
to Mark Ward, Designer,
The Real World, March–April 1985.

As the programme took its final shape and it became clear that there were few other options, the decision to use an actor in costume for Rampithecus was made. Initially, the idea was greeted with little enthusiasm from presenter Michael Rodd, and only some from Sue Jay. It was therefore important to enlist the Executive Producer's support. The next stage involved the researcher in locating artists' impressions of Ramapithecus for the use of make-up and wardrobe. Meanwhile, Kennedy discussed with the Contracts Department the feasibility of finding an actor who was available at short notice, the right shape (short and muscular in build), and willing to put up with the ordeal of a lengthy make-up and uncomfortable studio recording session. Contracts contacted the Ugly Agency whose clients – as the name implies – take on specialised and unusual walk-on roles.

At the same time, make-up and wardrobe, working from the picture, were liaising to determine the most convincing costume for

Studio layout for Dead as the Dodo?

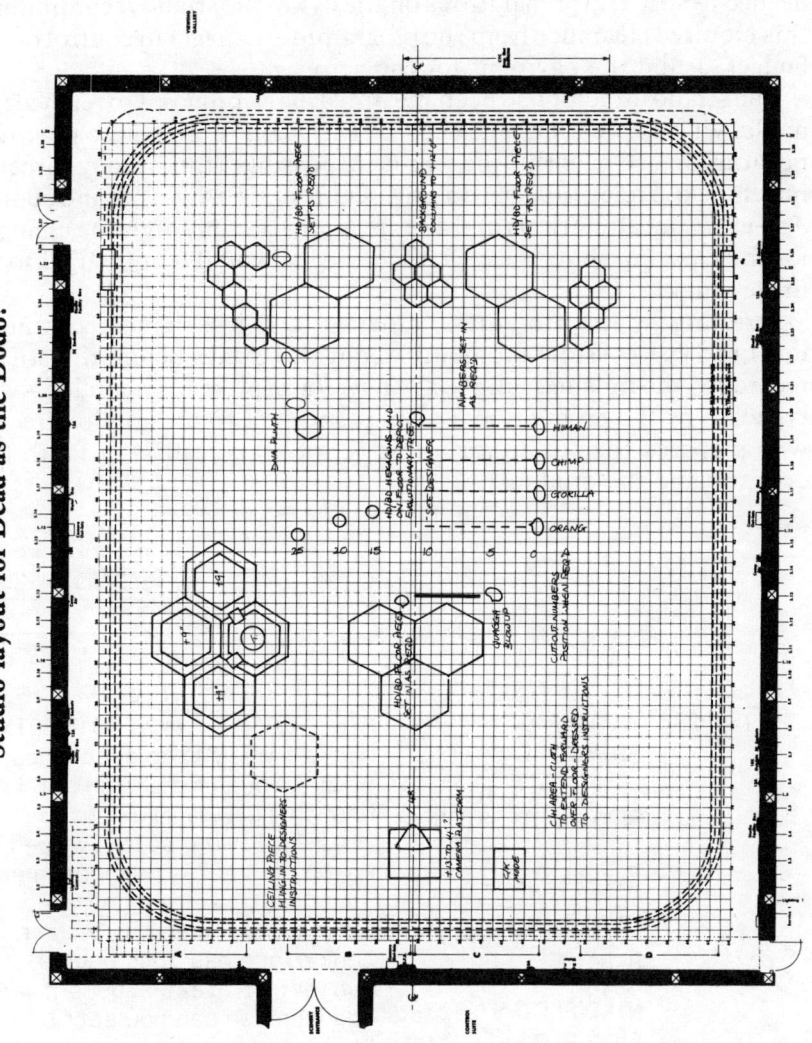

Ramapithecus. Within a day, the solution was presented – a skin-coloured bodysuit with head, hand and feet pieces, to be hired and built on with body hair. A second freelance make-up artist was needed to speed up preparations on the day of the studio recording and this required clearance from the programme manager in control of the budget, as did the payment for the actor.

The studio director had been informed of the proposal to replace the model with a live Ramapithecus, at the beginning of these practical negotiations. Once the idea proved possible, the studio director informed the relevant department; scenic design, lighting and sound. Any essential alterations in these areas (for example, lighting changes for the close-up shots a live Ramapithecus would require) had to be made quickly.

Scripting by the presenters, producer and researchers continued until the last possible moment. About three days before the studio recording, the finished script – the new Ramapithecus included – was typed up by the production assistant and sent to the studio director who prepared the studio recording script, in consultation with the designer and the producer.

```
                                                    ITEM 8
                                                    INTRODUCES
                                                    RAMAPITHECUS
                                                    DUR:
```

```
       FU                                      (LISTEN TO ¼" TAPE
21. CAM 2    MS MIKE IN          / MIKE TO CAM /      FOR DUBBING)
             ANIMAL LINE                   Man's family tree stretches
                                           back through time with our line
             TRACK BACK TO
             REVEAL MILESTONES  branching away from our
                                           closest living relatives – the
             END WITH 25M YEAR  chimp, gorilla, orangutan and
             MILESTONE                     so on over millions of years.
             F/G CR
             + ANIMAL LINE       But exactly when the breaks
             B/G                           took place has long been a
                                           subject of great argument – an
             MIKE BEGINS TO      argument we can now settle.
             WALK D/S CL         Let me introduce you to the
       CUT TO                    next clue in our detective
22. CAM 4    RAM'S FEET          story./
             TILT UP FROM
             FEET
```

```
                              MIKE V/O
                              This is Ramapithecus. He goes
                              back fourteen million years.
          CUT TO              We used to think he was a man.
23. CAM 2    2S RAM + MIKE    TO CAM More recently we have
             AS HE ARRIVES    not been so sure. We've always
          CUT TO              known the time he was around
24. CAM 1    CU TEETH         from
             IN MIKE'S HAND   MIKE V/O
          CUT TO              his teeth, which led us to
25. CAM 2    2S RAM + MIKE    believe that
```

MIKE TO CAM

MIKE WALKS BACK
TO ANIMAL LINE

Ramapithecus was more closely
related to us than to any of the
apes. And because we were

CRAB R +
PAN MIKE BACK
INTO ANIMAL LINE

certain that he was around
fourteen million years ago –
our family tree had to look like
this.

O/A RT:

/ / / / / / / / / / / TAPE STOP / / / / / / / / / / /

NB: SET FAMILY TREE

Phase 4: Editing and approval

The Ramapithecus sequence in *Dead as the Dodo?* survived the editing process after the studio recording in virtually the same form as it appears in the studio recording script. There were one or two changes in the presenters' scripts but apart from a shot of the animal line-up, dropped in during the editing, the sequence remained intact.

In fact, very little changed between the early outlines and the finished programme apart from the Ramapithecus episode. As early as six weeks before the studio recording and two months before the actual transmission date, the shape of the finished programme was already clear. Garfield Kennedy was able to define its specific features vividly enough to interest the press in 'trailing' its attractions.

10 April 1985

Mr Peter Jackson
Editor
Sunday Times Magazine
20 Gray's Inn Road
London WC1

Dear Peter

REAL WORLD

Please find enclosed press clippings as
background to our THE REAL WORLD network
science programme for planned transmission on
24 June 1985 at 7pm on ITV. I would suggest you
read the short San Francisco Examiner piece
first for accurate context. Taking the theme of
the cloning of the DNA of extinct animals we
will reveal the up to the minute work of a team
in Gainesville, Florida who have discovered
two eight-thousand-year-old human skulls in a
limestone-based swamp near Cape Canaveral.
These skulls have been found to carry
shrunken, but intact, brains. This material
has been successfully shown to contain
substantial quantities of clonable
mitochondrial DNA. Work continues to achieve
clones of short DNA strings — with all the
signs pointing to success, hopefully before
our programme is transmitted.

Our programme contains filmed sequences in
Berkeley with Dr Russel Higuchi and George
Poinar (who has worked with twenty-three-
million-year-old fruit flies encased in
amber). Additionally, a sequence with Dr
Jerold Lowenstein (see New Scientist article)
in San Francisco, and in San Diego Zoo with Dr
Ollie Ryder. Stills (colour transparencies
and black and white) for all these locations
are available.

On the East Coast we will cover the digs and
the laboratory work to unearth the human

specimens. Pictures of each stage of this work
— colour and black and white — are being
duplicated for us and can be made available to
you. I have already ordered dupes of selected
tranys for you and will continue to collect
further stills from other sources to complete
a fascinating story of scientific detective
work which we know will be a programme filled
with extraordinary surprises.

If you are interested in a piece to tie in with
our transmission (ie your magazine of the 23rd
June 1985) then we would be happy to supply
pictures, information and any article backed
by an exclusive collection of colour
pictures.

I would ask that you treat the above
information as confidential, subject to an
agreement to proceed on a co-operative basis
with TVS. We see no good reason not to share
our information with you, however, since it
can only be of benefit to both parties if the
idea grabs you as much as it grabbed us.

For information: THE REAL WORLD is an
occasional full network prime-time popular
science series on ITV. This will be our fourth
series and we have consistently achieved the
highest ratings for a factual programme on all
four networks. In the past we have been
associated with our very successful 3-D
transmission and the current series includes
the first programme ever to have smells on
world television. (We are issuing three and a
half million multiple "scratch and smell"
packs with TV Times).

I realise time is still on our side but if you
can come back to me soon with your reaction, I
would be very grateful. May I suggest that a
meeting between your Science Editor, Tony
Osman and our team (Michael Rodd, reporter;

Thelma Rumsey, researcher and myself) would
be a good way to move everything forward
quickly.

I look forward to your early reply.

Yours sincerely

GARFIELD KENNEDY
Producer/Director
THE REAL WORLD

NOTE: *The Sunday Times* did publish the article suggested here as 'Time to put the old brain to work again' pp. 42–48 on June 2nd for the rescheduled transmission of *Dead as the Dodo!* on June 10th 1985.

Phase 5: Transmission

Looking in this way at one small element in the production of a single programme may give some idea of the chronology and logic of the process. But it represents only a fraction of all the activities and decisions which go towards the finished programme. The Ramapithecus sequence in *Dead as the Dodo!* is presented as an important 'clue' in the 'detective story', establishing the significance of research on proteins as a basis from which to view the importance of work on DNA, in the quest for the origins of life itself. The inclusion of a representation of Lowenstein's discoveries is therefore crucial to the story the programme tells, but doubts remain about its succcess. Garfield Kennedy comments:

> I am not convinced now about the worth of putting an actor in the Ramapithecus role. If, in studio, the joke had really worked, then it would have been an excellent decision, lightening a quite heavy subject, but as it was it fell a little flat. That's one of the problems of studio – often your brave attempts which don't quite work, get transmitted.

The sequence attempts fidelity to a complex scientific argument, using a popular style which tries to entertain as it explains. The two aims are not necessarily irreconcilable but in this particular instance, there is an added problem. The sequence may work on a humorous level, but the fact that an actor is playing Ramapithecus amongst stuffed apes and chimpanzees and next to human presenters may also create some confusion. Ramapithecus is played by 'one of us' (an actor in a costume) but the script explains that 'poor old Ramapithecus isn't really one of us after all'. The method of presentation may, as Garfield Kennedy admits, cause confusion rather than clarity.

'Programmes without hairy gorillas will be given preferential consideration . . .'

Philip Geddes, Executive Producer, The Real World

Taking shape

During the production process, a shift of emphasis had occurred which took the focus away from the extinct animals and closer to the story of human evolution. The final running order of the programme as transmitted shows that some studio props and items of film have been lost and new elements (like the interview with Dr Phil Laipis) have been introduced. Nearly every surviving element has changed its importance in relation to other elements. The quagga has been completely displaced from the opening sequence and the programme now begins with the Gainesville skull, or Florida Brain, instead.

PAGE ONE
VTR: 29.5.1985
TXN: 10.6.1986

THE REAL WORLD — RUNNING ORDER
PROGRAMME 2 : 'DEAD AS THE DODO?'

ITEM	CONTENT	SOURCE	SOUND	R/T	
1.	STATION IDENT + OPENING TITLES	VTR	VTR	0'33"	
2.	INTRODUCTION				
2A.	FLORIDA BRAIN (1)	VTR	VTR+ ¼" TAPE		
2B.	SUE/LINK TO ASTEROIDS VTR	STUDIO CAP GEN	SUE	0'10"	
2C.	VTR: ASTEROIDS (1)	VTR	SUE V/O ¼" TAPE MIKE V/O		
2D.	MIKE/LINK DODO WINK VTR	STUDIO CENTRE CAP GEN	MIKE	0'10"	
2E.	DODO WINK VTR	VTR	¼" TAPE		
2F.	HEADLINES VTR	VTR	VTR	0'34"	
	MIKE + SUE/WIND UP INTRODUCTION	STUDIO CENTRE	MIKE SUE		
/ / / / / / / / / / / / TAPE STOP / / / / / / /					
3.	SUE/DINO DIORAMA (1)	STUDIO	SUE		
/ / / / / / / / / / / / / TAPE STOP / / / / / /					
4.	SUE/DINO DIORAMA (2)	CK AREA	SUE		
/ / / / / / / / / / / / / TAPE STOP / / / / / /					
5.	DNA VTR	VTR	VTR + MIKE V/O	0'22" avail.	

6.	MIKE/DNA DEMO	STUDIO PLINTH	MIKE		
	SAN DIEGO VTR	VTR	VTR	6'10"	
7.	SUE/STILLS SEQUENCE	STUDIO STILLS T/C SL.	SUE + MIKE		
/ / / / / / / / / / / / TAPE STOP / / / / / /					
8.	MIKE/INTRODUCES RAMAPITHECUS	STUDIO ANIMAL LINE	MIKE		
/ / / / / / / / / / / / TAPE STOP / / / / / /					
9.	MIKE/FAMILY TREE	ANIMAL LINE	MIKE		
	SUE/RAM'S JAW + TEST TUBES	DNA	SUE		
	MIKE/BACK REF	ANIMAL LINE	MIKE		
/ / / / / / / / / / / / TAPE STOP / / / / /					
10.	MIKE + SUE/FAMILY TREE	TREE + PLINTH	MIKE SUE		
	+ LOWENSTEIN VTR	VTR	SUE V/O + VTR	1'24"	
/ / / / / / / / / / / / / TAPE STOP / / / / /					
11.	SUE/LINK SWEDISH MUMMY	DNA PLINTH	SUE 1/4" TAPE		
	SWEDISH MUMMY VTR	VTR	VTR	0'52"	
	FLORIDA BRAIN (2) VTR	VTR	VTR + 1/4" TAPE	2'23"	
/ / / / / / / / / / / / TAPE STOP / / / / / /					
12.	SUE/INTERVIEW with DR. PHIL LAIPIS	INTERVIEW AREA	SUE + DR. LAIPIS		
	SUE/LINK FRUIT FLIES	STUDIO	SUE		
	FRUIT FLIES VTR	VTR	SUE V/O + VTR	2'22"	
/ / / / / / / / / / / / TAPE STOP / / / / / /					

ITEM	CONTENT	SOURCE	SOUND	R/T	
	SUE + MIKE/METEORITE	PLINTH T/C SL.	SUE MIKE		
	ASTEROID VTR	VTR	SUE V/O + ¼" TAPE		
/ / / / / / / / / / / / TAPE STOP / / / / / / /					
14.	SUE/WIND UP	CK AREA STILLS	SUE		
	DNA REPRISE VTR	VTR	SUE V/O + VTR		
	SUE/LINK DR'S COMMENT	CK AREA	SUE		
	DR. LAIPIS' COMMENT VT	VTR	VTR		
	WRAP UP STATEMENTS VT	VTR	VTR	0'31"	
/ / / / / / / / / / / / TAPE STOP / / / / / / /					
15.	MIKE/GENERAL WIND	CENTRE	MIKE		
	DODO WINK REPRISE	VTR	¼" TAPE		
	END SEQUENCE VTR	VTR	VTR	1'05"	

The pace of the programme may well in the end be somewhat breathless. This could be partly a result of the need to meet short deadlines or the need to compress a mass of material into a very small pre-determined space. It is also, however, a result of the need to tell a story and present an argument in a way which has an immediate appeal and which is readily accessible to the programme's viewers at a particular time of day.

We can also see the selection criteria which apparently determined the original choice of topics for the series exerting their pressure on the final presentation. The changes which occurred in the demonstration of DNA between studio script and recording can be explained according to the Galtung and Ruge criteria of 'meaningfulness' and 'personalisation'.

Item 6. DNA Demo. Michael Rodd. Voice-over. Camera 1. Close-up of DNA demo.

'This is human DNA. Each single strand of this cotton-wool like material contains all the chemical instructions which dictate everything about us from the colour of our eyes to the size of our feet.'

Clearly the intention was for Michael Rodd to undertake a simple experiment which involved drawing off a strand of DNA from a test-tube containing human DNA. This was thought sufficient to introduce the properties of DNA. But at rehearsals the concept of 'strands from cotton-wool like material' was dropped. The final version involved no 'strand pulling', and the concept of DNA was further simplified to:

> 'This is human DNA. In this sticky, viscous chemical are all the instructions which make up an individual, from the colour of their eyes to the size of their feet.'

'Strands', 'cotton-wool', and 'chemical instructions', were replaced by 'sticky', 'viscous', and simply 'instructions', in an attempt to simplify an obviously complex idea. Both versions, however, retain the statement that 'This is human DNA.' In actual fact it was mouse DNA. The 'meaningfulness' and 'personalisation', are achieved by means of a little poetic licence.

There is often some fine-tuning in the studio and in the final editing phase after the studio recording has been done. Pressure of time in the studio and the imperative of filling the transmission time to the precise second sometimes result in the excision of material. The material which is cut is rarely hard-won expensive props or visuals which have taken weeks of research and effort to produce. Sometimes it is an explanatory phrase or a sign-post for the viewer which has to be lost. In *Dead as the Dodo?* a scripted link was omitted in this way, on the grounds that it was redundant.

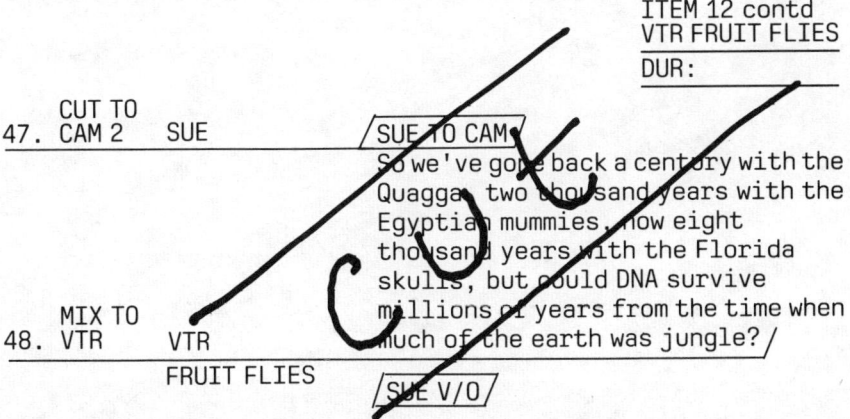

ITEM 12 contd
VTR FRUIT FLIES
DUR:

```
         CUT TO
47.      CAM 2      SUE              /SUE TO CAM/
                                     So we've gone back a century with the
                                     Quagga, two thousand years with the
                                     Egyptian mummies, now eight
                                     thousand years with the Florida
                                     skulls, but could DNA survive
         MIX TO                      millions of years from the time when
48.      VTR        VTR              much of the earth was jungle? /
         ─────────────────────────────────────────────────
                    FRUIT FLIES      /SUE V/O/
```

Similarly, a fairly subtle (but possibly libellous) reservation about Fred Hoyle's theories was cut:

```
                                        ITEM 13 contd
                                        LINK        VT+
                                        ASTEROID    VT
                                        DUR:
```

(55 on 4   BOOK   MIKE V/O

                            Professor Fred Hoyle has been
                            claiming for years that life came
                            from space ~~but up to now he has been~~
56. CAM 3   MIKE   *cut* ~~regarded as pretty way out~~ /

                            / MIKE TO CAM /

                            Who knows? Perhaps Professor Hoyle
57. CUT T/C SLIDE   is right /
              Fruit-Fly
                            / MIKE V/O /

It was not by any means essential to the argument, but its loss meant that his case was given more authority by being presented without comment. In the end, the decisions made in the production process inevitably affect the shape and impact of the finished programme. They also determine the form which the scientific argument takes.

5

Making Sense of Science

The rhetoric of *The Real World*
Opening moves
Words and pictures
Presenters and people
Wit and wisdom

Dead as the Dodo? raises a multitude of complex scientific issues, most of which are outside the experience and knowledge of the majority of viewers. So how does the programme go about presenting and explaining these? What television techniques does it use to get the attention of viewers and draw them in?

In this chapter we investigate how sounds and images are combined with each other to create structures of meaning. The sounds we examine include presenters' voice-overs, music and special effects. The images include computer-generated graphics, photographs, drawings, captions, models, location film, studio props and the presenters. We also look at how sequences of sounds and images create particular rhythms and texture for the narrative exposition. And we explore the way in which the viewer is drawn into the narrative by the promise of an exciting quest for scientific knowledge.

The rhetoric of *The Real World*

How many times in one evening's continuous television viewing are you likely to be faced with a blank screen? In all probability the answer is 'not at all', for producers are constrained by television's need constantly to fill the screen. Yet in *Dead as the Dodo?* the screen is blank, albeit for a split second, on two occasions. But it is in the nature of television that even the gaps must have significance, and so the first occasion (a fade) follows Michael Rodd's announcement that 'The quagga mare died alone in the zoo in 1883'; and the second comes when we learn of the fate of the fruit-fly as it lands on a resinous tree: 'it wasn't a very good idea'. The fade to blackness signifies death.

For the rest of the programme, though there may be moments when no one speaks and occasions when music is not played, there are no moments when the eye is ever allowed to rest, as the programme's frenetic activity demands that the viewer follow and make sense of a multitude of successive images.

If activity is the first rule of television, then variety is arguably the second. The programme is less than 26 minutes long and the quagga is but one part of it. Yet we see a cardboard cut-out of a quagga in the studio, black and white stills of old quaggas and young quaggas, coloured illustrations of quaggas, pieces of quagga tissue, and even film of living animals that in some way resemble quaggas.

This is television's dilemma when it seeks to present issues that are not in themselves essentially visual. The producer of a popular science programme may fear losing the audience because they may not easily follow difficult scientific concepts. But there is also a fear of losing them through boredom, and so the duration of an image on the screen must be brief. The average shot-length in *Dead as the Dodo!* is a mere 6 seconds.

Jerry Mander suggests that we carry out a simple test by putting on our televisions and counting the number of times that a cut, a zoom, a voice-over, captions or other 'technical events' occur. The 45 second section between the title-sequence and Michael Rodd's first appearance contains more than a dozen 'technical events' as the camera zooms in, zooms out, cuts from still to scientist, from scientist's face to scientist's hand, from California to the studio.

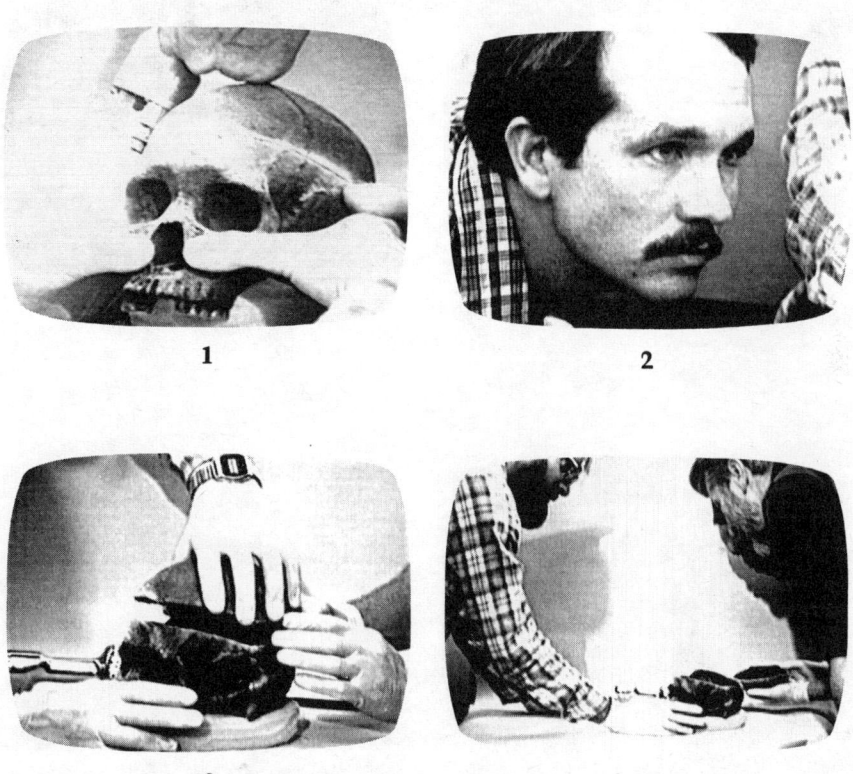

1

2

3

4

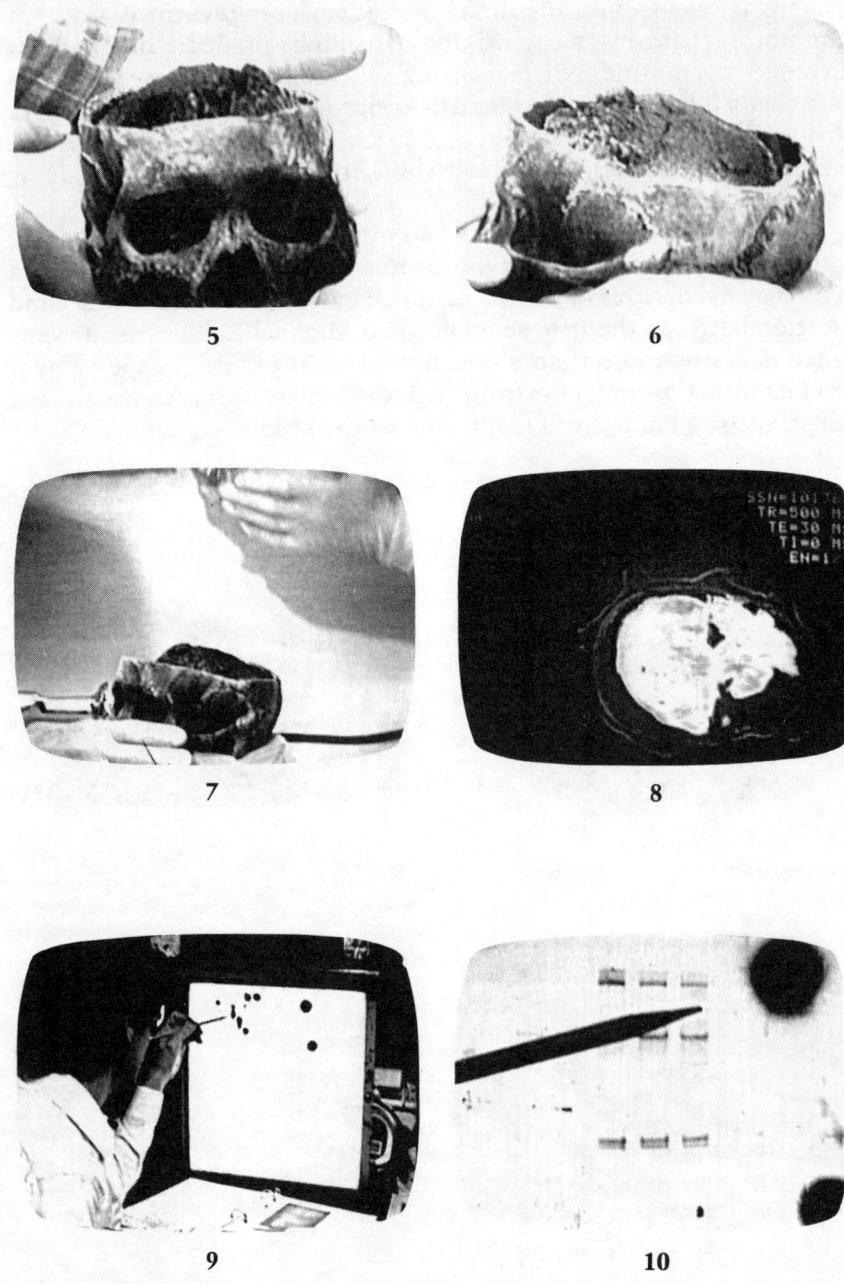

5

6

7

8

9

10

11   12

The presentational effort in such a sequence aims to do much more than simply avoid boredom. As in a tabloid newspaper, such sequences use fragments which in themselves mean very little to create a mosaic which offers a significant and satisfying pattern. It is a kind of televisual journalese which uses short, punchy sentences, avoids jargon and creates plenty of variety. The visual and acoustic techniques of television are used in a sophisticated way to compress a lot of information into very little space. The result is a sequence of extreme density.

Yet to viewers there is nothing technical or unnatural in this. What we perceive is a 'seamless flow'. We have become so accustomed to having the world mediated for us in this way that the evidence of our own senses can sometimes seem inadequate. Try watching a live sporting event after experiencing a surfeit of television coverage. The natural perspective of the spectator can seem woefully inadequate and even slightly alien.

Opening moves

But television can and sometimes does establish an altogether different relationship with its audience. Instead of spoon-feeding, it can challenge. Instead of concealing its own artifice, it can highlight the techniques that make it different from other media. Consider the title-sequence of *The Real World*. Although this sequence is now over five years old and has been upstaged by new digital techniques, it still captures the idea of what the producer, Garfield Kennedy, calls 'a modern journey of discovery'.

A computer graphics grid appears two-dimensionally. Three-dimensionally it transforms into a tunnel through which the viewer journeys, veering quickly right, then left, as if on some manic subway. The subway walls are lined not with advertising hoardings but tantalising fragments of numbers in red and white light. Electronic music directs and reinforces our attention, building in intensity as it proceeds. The destination we reach is a vast space with a roof: we see vertical yellow lines with a sky at the centre. In the centre of the horizon appears a succession of vertical laboratory images presented in a digitised form as if through an X-ray, or some modern scanner. Finally, the yellow vertical lines reappear and reveal themselves as the base of the three-dimensional 'WORLD'.

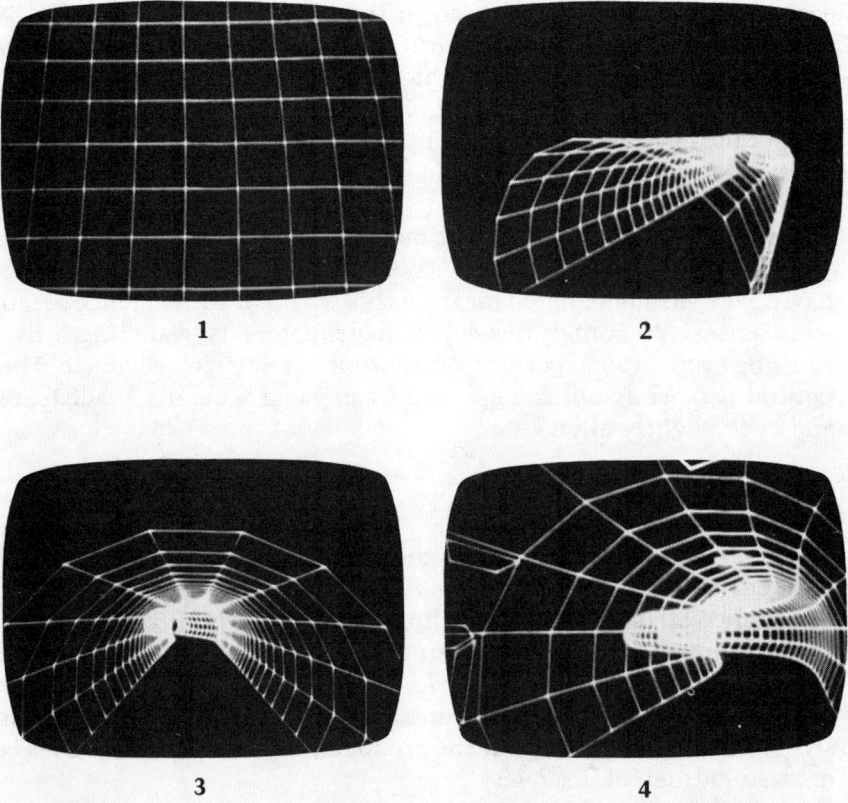

1   2

3   4

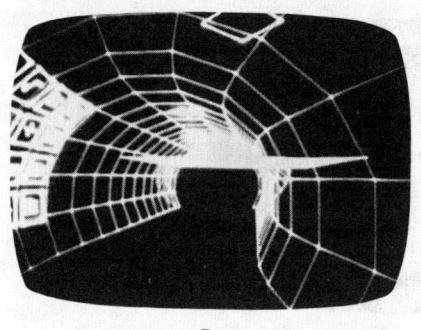

5

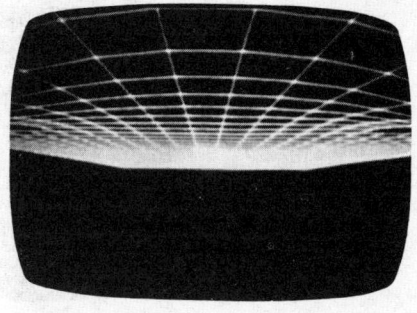

6

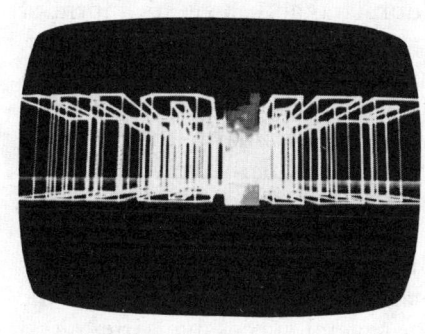

7

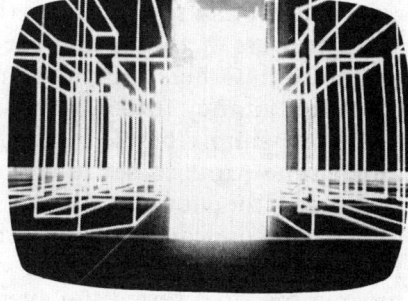

8

9

10

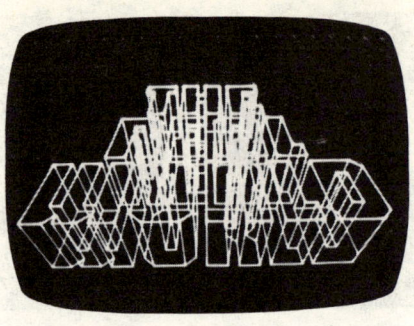

11

Is *this* the 'real world'? What is denoted is a grid, a tunnel, some numbers, movement. The precise connotations are for the viewer to decide. But the musical crescendo unmistakably suggests a form of achievement and resolution as the journey comes to its conclusion. Some viewers might register such notions as speed, the future, high technology. Others might construct a complex narrative of a computer journey into a brave new world. For many, the connotations will simply be of the opening of a popular, lively television programme: time to settle down and pay attention. The choice is apparently the viewer's.

The open-endedness of meaning in this title-sequence also stems from the fact that it has to be versatile enough to work for all the programmes in a series and even for several successive series. As a result, it is very abstract. Such sequences are retained through several series not simply because they are expensive to produce but also because they do a great deal of work in identifying the programme in order to create audience loyalty. The title-sequence is the moment when viewers are invited in and where their commitment to watching the programme must occur. As in many successful advertisements, the openness to different interpretations invites viewers to participate in a semantic dialogue.

Not so the rest of the programme, where the presenters' words and carefully chosen musical cues delimit the range of possible meanings of any image or set of images (e.g. the eerie music used during the mummies sequence). Implicit in the title-sequence is an intelligent participative viewer. Implicit in the rest of the programme is a viewer who has to be cajoled and constantly amused. Dominant in creating this impression is the relationship between sound and image.

Words and pictures

The images at first glance appear to illustrate the soundtrack. When human DNA is mentioned we see it in a test-tube; when a dinosaur is mentioned one inevitably appears. Yet the words speak for themselves and the images provide no elaboration. The sight of DNA in a test-tube is uninformative and there can be few people who cannot mentally conjure up a dinosaur at the mention of the word. The words, in fact, anchor the pictures, give some context in which the images can be interpreted. So the zoo montage with its zany music is given significance by the phrase 'modern Noah's ark'. But the cutting of the film to the rhythm of the music also creates a kind of animal ballet which is both aesthetic and amusing in itself.

Even when the images are rather more specific the words still dominate the pictures. Constantly, tiny musical cues or 'stings' attract the viewer's attention and suggest the preferred way of 'reading' the images.

Vision   **Sound**

– '(Higuchi) identified a solvent'

– 'and added bacteria'

Presenters and people

Popular television thrives on people. *Dead as the Dodo?* is no exception. To hold our attention we have two presenters, one male, one female. They rarely appear without props, and both are frequently used only as voice-over. They sometimes appear together and on one occasion share the screen with a cardboard quagga. By directly addressing the camera, full face, both are presented as trustworthy and friendly. Michael Rodd, the dominant presenter, leans forward in a confidential manner, sure of his relationship with the viewer.

The presenters, however, are not the only people to appear in *Dead as the Dodo?*. Several scientists are shown presenting their expert testimony. Ryder, though not the most eminent, is clearly the most acceptable in televisual terms. He makes two extended appearances: the first time he is used, partly in voice-over, for the zoo montage; the second time he earns himself a very large close-up. In the latter sequence, his open direct gaze stands up well to television's relentless examination.

Not so the suave Dr Lowenstein.

Dr Ryder

Dr Lowenstein

His blinking eyes and awareness of the camera make him appear less confident. He is therefore shown mainly in mid-shot, supported by his immaculate clothing and a collection of skulls which serve as an unacknowledged backcloth.

Higuchi similarly merits a mid-shot, bolstered by the technology of his laboratory which lends him authority. He looks altogether too young and unprepossessing to be a television scientist. Poinar is interesting enough but his discoveries are yet to come and he can therefore hardly merit much television time.

Dr Higuchi

Dr Poinar

Perhaps the most revealing presentation is of Dr Laipis. Away from the tools of his trade, in a studio interview with Sue Jay, he provides something of a problem. Without the authority conferred by his own environment he appears to have little of great importance to say. Consequently, the camera moves restlessly from Jay to Laipis, from Jay's back to Laipis' back, zooming in and out, in an attempt to create the authentic feel of lively dialogue.

Sue Jay

Dr Laipis

The Laipis interview is also unusual in that it presents a scientist with a very human face. Television scientists are rarely presented in a context which allows them to express such personal emotion. Yet here Dr Laipis is interviewed in the kind of breathless way that occurs when an athlete has just won an event. It is very much a 'How Do You Feel?' interview as Sue Jay asks him to 'describe that moment when you realised that what you've got is not just a lump of earth clogging up the skull, but a real brain'.

Even the scientific process assumes a rather different appearance here. The metaphor of trying to recreate the *Hamlet* soliloquy from one isolated line, however successful as a means of describing the search for a complete DNA picture, tunes in neatly with the programme's own extended metaphor of the detective story. It also invites us to see the scientist as a man of letters as well as a specialist in his own field.

Wit and wisdom

Dead as the Dodo? constantly demonstrates television's capacity to make interpretative demands on viewers and to involve them in shared jokes. As Garfield Kennedy puts it, 'If you entertain people and hold their attention through wit, then you can actually tell them more complex things.' The use of a blank screen mentioned earlier is one example of this. There are also the dissolves of skulls, each taken from different angles, used to illustrate the concept of cloning or the flight of the fruit-fly dramatised by the camera's crazy journey through the trees.

Dead as the Dodo?, like most popular science programmes on television, has a restlessness which occasionally borders on neurosis. It moves from image to image, taking what is visually appealing in its subject matter and discarding the rest. It relies on acoustic signals to establish mood and pace or to signal a preferred 'reading' of the programme.

Is this way of presenting science inevitable? From an educational point of view, the danger is that the popular science programme may persuade people that they understand science more than they actually do. There is certainly some evidence from the responses of viewers that this is the case. It may make science seem fun and exciting but it could, unfortunately, make the work of educators more rather than less difficult. What difficulties may be raised for a more serious look at such areas as human genealogy, creation and evolution, DNA, cloning and the biochemistry of animals after *Dead as the Dodo?* A weeping Ramapithecus and a winking dodo are hard acts to follow.

6
Telling Stories

A network of narratives
Content: evolution and genetics
Method: exposition and rhetoric
The narrative framework: three story forms

The 'Who shot JR?' syndrome is central to an understanding of how most television works and why most people watch it. Stories are as fundamental to television programmes as they are to novels. Even those documentaries which claim to be following events rather than leading viewers through a story have many formal characteristics similar to fiction. Science programmes, as much as soap operas, tell a story with a beginning, a middle and an end.

The smoothness of the finished programme sometimes disguises the diversity of elements within it and the intricate ways in which they may be woven together. *Dead as the Dodo?* is the result, according to Garfield Kennedy's estimate, of two or three *million* decisions. Although Thelma Rumsey, the Researcher, felt retrospectively that the finished programme contained 'two ideas too many', it nevertheless achieves an impressive continuity and flow during its 26 minutes' duration.

At the same time, the constant forward thrust of the programme may conceal the fact that many different things are being said and many different stories being told. The most modern scientific information is presented through the medium of television, one of its own recent products. But, paradoxically, it communicates this information through one of the oldest story forms or myths. This does not mean that producers or viewers are consciously aware

of a mythical dimension, simply that there is a limited number
of ways in which stories can be told. This chapter examines the main
narrative strands and the way they interact within the programme.

A network of narratives

Having watched *Dead as the Dodo?* viewers may be puzzled about
the nature and significance of DNA, somewhat confused about man's
origins and perhaps a little bewildered by the possibility of cloning
mammoths. Some uncertainty is, of course, inevitable and perhaps
desirable in any learning process. In any case, the programme is
generally educative rather than educational in the strict sense.
However, these questions are the substance of the programme's
narrative; and narrative is clearly central, as we are constantly
reminded by the presenters. They invite us to 'take the first step
in tonight's story'. But if this framing device of offering *Dead
as the Dodo?* as a detective story is the most obvious aspect of
narrative in the programme it is not the only one. The programme
is in fact a network of narratives.

'Story' is a term which is often used in the media to refer both to the
content of an item ('finding a story') and to the method of its telling.
But the distinction is a little misleading in that stories do not simply
occur, but are told. We may forget that the very act of communicating
apparently 'solid' information involves the shaping of that information into a 'story'; and the way we tell the story materially affects the
way we understand the information.

We have already discussed how stories are selected and filtered for
television science programmes in much the same way as occurs with
news items. In a similar way, we have suggested how science itself is
not simply a body of knowledge or facts but a continuing debate
between competing theories about what is known. In other words,
both television science and science in general are, in their different
ways, as concerned with the perspective or 'angle' created as with the
simple information.

In *Dead as the Dodo?* we have to deal with two substantial story
elements. One of these concerns the current state of knowledge about
evolution while the other concerns genetics. These are the 'what?' of
the programme and may be best thought of as content. In addition to
these two main elements, there are also two distinct and sometimes
competing narrative methods to be found. One of these relies on a
standard form of classical exposition. The other depends more on

forms of demonstration, proof and persuasion which we can call televisual rhetoric.

At the same time, there are three different forms of story-telling or narrative frameworks which are fairly typical of popular television. We have called these *the heroic conquest story, the domestic drama story* and *the detective story*.

Content: evolution and genetics

To begin with, there are two narrative strands that, in a sense, pre-exist the screening of the programme itself. The first concerns evolution and extinction, the raw material upon which all the other narratives are based. It places significant evolutionary events in a particular chronological order. This order, however, is disturbed by the programme's other narrative threads and requires a great deal of careful teasing out.

The story begins when a primitive life-form hitches a lift on a meteor and lands 60 million years later on Earth:

3 000 000 000 years ago :	meteor lands on Earth – life begins?
65 000 000 years ago* :	extinction of the dinosaur
23 000 000 years ago :	demise of one fruit-fly
14 000 000 years ago :	extinction of Ramapithecus
10 000 000 years ago :	man diverges from orang-utan
4 000 000 years ago :	man diverges from gorillas and chimps
8 000 years ago :	two humans die in a Florida swamp
2 000 years ago :	an Egyptian dies and is mummified
about 300 years ago* :	extinction of the dodo
about 100 years ago :	extinction of the quagga

* dates not available from television programme

(The story, of course, does not end there, and there is a light-hearted glance at life in the future with the cloned dodo.) The implications for both the producer and the viewer are apparent when one remembers that this account of evolution is just one fragment of a programme that occupies less than 26 minutes.

The programme on the whole follows this chronological sequence, but in reverse order. The search for clonable DNA begins with relatively recent material in the quagga (100 years old) and progresses through Ramapithecus (14 million years old) to the fruit-flies in amber (23 million years old). But between Ramapithecus and the fruit-flies, we are taken out of sequence to meet the Egyptian mummies (2,000 years old) and the Gainesville skulls (8,000 years old). The consequence of this, at least for one group of A-level students, is confusion:

Viewer 1	They kept jumping about, very bitty. Then right at the end saying about the fruit-fly? Shouldn't that have been at the beginning?
Viewer 2	Did we really have to know about the fruit-fly anyway?
Viewer 1	Because they haven't done anything with it.
Viewer 3	They were doing it in chronological order weren't they?
Viewer 1 & 2	No it didn't! (*sic*)
Viewer 1	It jumped about all over the place, 'cos he said about that 'donkey thing', then 'Let's look here and see about him'.

The sheer vastness of the evolutionary subject-matter contrasts strongly with the scale of the second narrative strand where we are concerned, amongst other things, with the DNA in the protein of the teeth of one ape. It is the story of the search for DNA in dead tissue and the development of a procedure for cloning. It might perhaps begin with the publication in 1858 of Darwin's, *On the Origin of Species. The Real World*, however, focuses on the contemporary world, and so we begin in 1979.

1979 : Reinhold Rau retrieves quagga tissue in S Africa

1982 : Dr Oliver Ryder in California receives quagga tissue

1982 : Dr Jerold Lowenstein settles the Ramapithecus issue in Rome

1984 : Dr Russell Higuchi extracts DNA from quagga

1984 : 8,000 year old human skulls found in Florida

1985 : DNA cloned from mummy by Swedish scientists

1985 : George Poinar investigates the fruit-fly

We have moved from dinosaurs and dodos to geneticists and biochemists, from outer space to West Coast USA, from the beginning of time to six years in the twentieth century. Though these stories are intertwined in the programme, they come from different contexts outside it and make divergent demands upon both the producer and the viewer.

For the viewer who watches the finished programme the issues that make up these stories are apparently settled (unless he or she brings prior knowledge to bear). The producer, however, in devising the programme has to make choices, just as scientists do. Which are the crucial discoveries? Which view of the past and the future has most authority and validity?

Method: exposition and rhetoric

When choices have been made about which elements are to be included in the finished programme, their original chronological sequence is inevitably abandoned. Instead, they are subordinated to the programme's need to present a clear and coherent narrative line. This narrative line is the means by which the whole programme is ordered. It consists of two complementary (but sometimes conflicting) aspects: the story or 'what next?' aspect and the argument or exposition, which is concerned with the 'how?' and 'why?' of the narrative.

In one way, the line follows a pattern similar to the traditional structure of classical exposition:

1	INTRODUCTION	designed to capture attention – the skull, the stars, a mummy and the quagga
2	PRESENTATION OF PROBLEM	a) to trace the origins of life b) to clone extinct creatures
3	DIVISION OF ARGUMENT INTO MANAGEABLE PARTS	quagga/Ramapithecus/human brain/fruit-fly
4	CONFIRMATION OF ARGUMENT	a) George Poinar develops the idea of man's origins in space b) Phil Laipis offers the possibility of mammoths in Rocky Mountain Park

5   SUMMING UP

a) Sue Jay: 'If all life came from one original source that's a real eye-opener'.

b) Michael Rodd: 'The next time you find yourself face to face with a dodo, remember we did warn you'.

But at the same time, the manner in which it is presented is peculiarly televisual. Musical 'stings' constantly work towards attracting attention or reinforcing particular feelings subconsciously. The credentials of the various scientists are established by showing them surrounded by the tools of their trade. The validity of *Nature*'s article on cloning from a mummy is established by contrasting it with the *Examiner* ('an American newspaper famous for its exaggeration'). The hysterical cover of the latter and the subdued front page of the former are all we see through captioned photographs.

When the DNA of the quagga is compared to that of a living zebra we see a row of capitals above a row of dots interspersed with some capitals, and hear 'The comparatively few letters show where the DNA of today's zebra does not correspond with that of its closely linked relative'. The fact that the significance of the letters themselves is incomprehensible to the vast majority of the viewing public does not matter. We are offered a clear visual contrast which acts as a token for a scientific test and demands our trust. We should remember, though, Neil Ryder's warning about the presentation of arguments on television: 'A visual demonstration is not a test. No argument on TV is complete or safe' (Ryder, 1982, p. 58).

These visual demonstrations often provide quick answers to specific questions. But do they clarify the programme's argument? In the end, we have to ask whether the attempt to 'unravel the mystery of our past' (Sue Jay) has actually succeeded. What do we now know about the origins of human life (or even animal life) or about the real potential of cloning? Can we, at the end of the programme, honestly answer more fully the question 'where did we come from?' (Michael Rodd)? The rhetoric of the programme would certainly have us believe so.

The narrative framework: three story forms

The *heroic conquest story*, as we shall call it, can be traced to a traditional story form. Throughout history, popular stories have been based on simple and familiar patterns. These stories have many forms and variants but they share recurrent features. Such patterns can be found as much in modern television as in traditional folk-tales. They are by no means deliberately drawn upon by programme makers nor made explicit in the programmes themselves; and it follows that they are not apparent to many viewers (unless they happen to be versed in structuralist analysis). But the traces of ancient story forms are still present in accounts of modern man. The mythical elements of the story in *Dead as the Dodo?* are easily recognisable; some elements, such as the Frankenstein myth, were even acknowledged openly by the programme team.

---

1   The quest is established: in this case, the search for the origins of life.

2   A wise man or elder (Michael Rodd) sends out a number of heroes to accomplish this task. The heroes include the viewer, Jerold Lowenstein, and Russell Higuchi.

3   When difficulties are encountered, magic is brought to bear (in this case, the magic of biochemistry and genetics).

4   The heroes face a series of increasingly difficult tasks (to clone DNA from the quagga, a human, and the fruit-fly).

5   Despite failures (the case of the baby mammoth) the heroes overcome all odds.

6   The heroes (Laipis, Ryder, Poinar, Lowenstein) return. (In particular, Laipis actually journeys from Florida to England to tell of his conquest.)

7   The story is neatly closed with the wise man's moral.

The second narrative framework, the *domestic drama story*, works be reducing large-scale theoretical issues to small-scale personal episodes or intimate domestic microdramas. This is one of the characteristic ways in which popular television works, as anyone will realise who remembers how in the Westland Affair in 1986 complex economic and political issues were translated by the media into a fist-fight between Heseltine and Brittan. As Garfield Kennedy himself says, 'In fact, it's like a soap opera: people think "Hang on, I'm interested – what is this about?"'

So in *Dead as the Dodo?*, research into the quagga is represented as a friendly relationship between Ryder and Higuchi. The former sent the quagga tissue to the latter because he himself found it 'too hot to handle'. Investigations into Ramapithecus are presented as the achievement of one man, suave Dr Jerold Lowenstein, a doctor of medicine for whom, one might almost think, genetic research is a serious 'hobby'. When Lowenstein tries to credit others with similar success he is told by Rodd that his work is 'fundamental'. Clearly the role of the individual protagonist is important in this story.

The viewer's interest must be held at all costs: horror (the sawing of the skull), humour (Ramapithecus), fantasy (the cloning of the dodo), and animal interest (San Diego Zoo) are all used. But perhaps the best example of this particular strand of story can be seen in the interview with Dr Laipis at the end of the programme. Sue Jay is talking to a scientist who is involved in crucial research with obvious ethical implications. Her first question, however, demands a personal and emotional response: 'Phil, can I ask you to describe that moment when you realised that what you've got is not just a lump of earth clogging up the skull, but a real brain?'

The third and final narrative framework invites viewers to take part in a sort of *detective story*. There are numerous verbal references to this detective framework.

'first step in tonight's story . . .'
'next link in our detective story . . .'
'new evidence . . .'
'unravel the mystery . . .'
'next clue in our detective story . . .' (three times)

There is even a 'criminal', that pervasive con-man Ramapithecus ('how long can he go on pretending?') and there is no shortage of corpses. The viewer is cast in the role of detective alongside the presenter in an attempt to discover 'who dunnit?'

However, for some viewers the mystery is unsolved and the enigmas remain. Indeed, many might still be asking 'who dunwhat?' The journey is everything, the arrival nothing. The question remains: what *are* the links between DNA, cloning and the origins of human life? The variety of narrative strands certainly provides a richness of texture and a colourful framework for the 'gosh! factors' to work within. The big question is whether they help in clarifying and explaining the scientific issues which the programme raises.

AUDIENCES

How do audiences respond?

The very word 'audiences' is problematic. It draws immediate attention to some of the most basic problems in discussing how television is used. It is an inadequate word because, like 'viewers' it focuses on only one of the perceptual channels or senses involved in the process. We have no word which describes the *activity* of watching television. Whilst 'reading' has a clear sense of *doing* rather than just *receiving*, all of our descriptions of viewing seem to imply some form of passivity.

This is not just a question of vocabulary: the words themselves have a history which relates to assumptions about what television *does to* people, rather than what they do with it. These assumptions are found in a great deal of current discussion about the effects of television, especially where children are concerned (as in the 1983 DES Report). They can also be seen at work even in more sophisticated accounts of television audiences:

> TV's regime of vision is less intense than cinema's: it is a regime of the glance rather than the gaze. The gaze implies a concentration of the spectator's activity into that of looking, the glance implies that no extraordinary effort is being invested in the activity of looking. The very terms we habitually use to designate the person who watches TV or the cinema screen tend to indicate this difference. The cinema-looker is a spectator: caught by the projection yet separate from its illusion. The TV-looker is a viewer, casting a lazy eye over proceedings, keeping an eye on events, or, as the slightly archaic designation had it, 'looking in'.   (Ellis, 1982, p. 137).

Audiences are actually part of the institution of television, both in terms of how they are constructed and in terms of how they use and respond to it. We have already examined how the audience for *The Real World* is *expected* to react and respond in certain ways. But we have also suggested that the actual interaction between audiences and programmes is an unpredictable and sometimes surprising process. Richard Dyer reminds us that audiences are ultimately implicated in representation. There is no such thing as a programme without an audience nor a set of meanings which are fixed within a 'text'.

Representation should also make us think of the *audience*. In this inflection, we should include ourselves: what does this programme represent to me; what does it mean to other people who watch it? We often leave this stage out of account; especially, I regret to say, in education. Teachers often try to get pupils and students to see what a programme represents 'ideally' (i.e. as *teachers* understand it) without also finding out what it represents to them. We need to learn to listen better – especially to children – to understand what sense they in turn make out of the work represented to them.

(Lusted & Drummond, 1985, p. 42)

We should now look, therefore, at how audiences of *The Real World* actually do respond to it and what sort of sense they make of it. Before we do so, however, we need to take a small step backwards to look at how the programme gets an audience in the first place and how the audience is constructed by the programme. This means looking at how the ITV network operates, how regional and network programmes are blended into the schedules and how programmes relate to advertisements.

The television industry has its own mechanism for measuring audience loyalty and assessing their reactions. The Broadcasters' Audience Research Board provides quantitative data for any given programme. It is based on returns from a representative panel of 3,000 computer-linked homes for: gross viewing figures (expressed in thousands); share of total audience; and for 'TVR' (which derives from the other two figures). The panel survey also provides a much more detailed breakdown of viewing by social class, age and gender.

On top of this, some qualitative information about responses and attitudes is also available from the BARB Reaction Service, based on a regular questionnaire to the same panel. This contains general questions as well as specific ones added by individual television companies. Finally, both the BBC and IBA (and, more recently, even some of the ITV companies themselves) have established their own Research Departments which carry out specially commissioned work, often by means of interviews and discussion groups.

The Reaction Service produced an Appreciation Index (the AI) which is expressed as a percentage and gives a sense of audience satisfaction, as against indicating the number of television sets switched on at the time of transmission. Very few of any channel's Top Ten rated programmes also achieve Top Ten AIs. Typically, high AIs go to successful comedy shows, and royalty and animal programmes, while continuous serials achieve the high numerical scores.

A programme has succeeded if it registers high viewing figures and high AIs. If the viewing figures are high but the AI low, a regular but indifferent audience is implied. The reverse is often achieved by quality minority programming (often on Sundays). If both measures are low, then something has gone wrong. An AI percentage below 25 is discounted, under 50 is suspect and over 80 is outstanding. Broadcasters do take notice of these figures and they have an effect on programme planning and scheduling. But they always need to be interpreted with care.

Having examined the structures which determine programmes and deliver them to audiences, we can then explore audience responses in more detail. The final chapter discusses the context in which audiences make television programmes meaningful, and reveals something of their resilience when faced with high-powered messages. If audiences are, as we have suggested, a crucial part of the institution of television, then we need to consider the implications of their responses. They matter not merely for producers of programmes but also for those who ultimately make sense of them. In the end, the television programme which is 'consumed' by viewers is not actually the meal which is offered: it is only the menu from which audiences choose.

7

Advertising and Audiences

Money matters
Programmes, audiences and advertising
The Real World audience

Why is *The Real World* like it is? One explanation is that it is determined by purely commercial motives. This explanation starts from the premise that all ITV companies are in business to make money for their employees, directors and shareholders; and since their main source of income is from advertising, they will inevitably seek to maximise their advertising revenues. Therefore they will need to make programmes able to host the advertisements which seek to appeal to the widest possible market. So the only programmes made will be those with mass appeal.

Such a crude view of the economies of television needs to be modified; there are other constraints at work which ensure that not all programmes are made simply to attract the largest possible audiences. The current system of taxing ITV advertising revenue means that other sources of income may actually be more profitable; the IBA itself influences ITV programming, and programme makers, too, clearly have their own motives and interests.

Most important (and perhaps most surprising) is the fact that TVS makes more money than all the other Regional ITV companies (and more than some of the Majors) by attracting fewer viewers to the programmes it shows. How is it that with audiences about 15% lower than the ITV average it can charge rates 50% higher to advertisers? What effect does this have on TVS' revenues and on programmes?

Establishing links between programmes and the economic conditions which they depend on is notoriously difficult. Nor is it always clear how this actually helps us to understand the programmes. This chapter shows how examining the links between programmes, advertisements and audiences can help us towards an understanding of *The Real World*.

Money matters

It is a truism of the television system that money makes programmes and programmes make money. What is of particular interest is exactly how this occurs. How much money should be spent on making programmes and how much can be generated by their distribution are matters of disagreement and debate within the industry. They are the basic questions which define the economics of television.

Despite some obvious differences, both the BBC and ITV companies are dependent on similar economic imperatives. The former depends almost exclusively on the revenue raised from licence-fees, the latter on that raised from advertisements.

Undoubtedly, the primary function of a television company is to make programmes for its viewers. No television company could sustain its levels of production if its output did not achieve the necessary viewing figures. It is viewers who pay for programmes, whether through the licence-fee or through the purchase of heavily advertised consumer goods. In the financial year which ended in 1987, TVS earned 83% (over £143m) of its turnover from television advertising sales. This amounts to nearly 11% of total ITV network revenue. Even so, TVS is rather less dependent on advertising as a proportion of total revenue than most of the ITV companies.

There is within the industry a constant tension between the demands of accounting and those of programme making. The former naturally insists on economies, while the latter seeks ways of achieving the best quality of programmes which money can buy. This tension becomes more acute when government policy and technological change instil uncertainty about the traditional means of financing the 'comfortable duopoly' of broadcasting.

The Peacock Report has raised new anxieties for broadcasters in the form of a recommendation that they should in future accept a 40% quota of programmes from 'independent' producers. Even though the figure has been revised down to a general target of 25%, there is still justified concern about the likely effects of such a change in the structure of programming. Similarly, the notion of a 'free-for-all' franchise competition has caused some disquiet, even though current franchises have been extended by three years to 1992. Fears of limited advertising being carried by the BBC have not been completely allayed.

The Peacock Committee also concluded that broadcasting should 'move towards a sophisticated market system based on consumer sovereignty' but with special provision for public service programmes. The possible abolition of the licence-fee and the introduction of subscription for BBC progammes in the 1990s is a drastic prospect. It would probably have the effect of detaching ITV entirely from its links with the BBC (through the shared ethos of public service broadcasting) and put it into direct competition with other purely commercial operations. On top of this, the new media 'watchdog' announced by Douglas Hurd, the prospect of a Fifth Channel and the possible selling off of Channel 4 have all conspired to concentrate the minds of anyone in broadcasting with a predisposition towards complacency.

Finally, the threat of competition from the new cable and satellite technologies poses further problems for the stability of broadcasting. New means of distribution and types of programming may prove attractive to financiers and advertisers. The new media may take a share of what is usually believed to be a limited supply of advertising revenue, especially if they can offer more precisely defined audiences than traditional broadcasting.

In these circumstances, new strategies have to be devised. TVS has responded to the new economic situation in two main ways, both of which depend on generating additional income from sources other than television advertising.

Firstly, it has raised capital from stock issues. The initial flotation in 1984 raised £8m. Two years later, the company raised an additional £19.3m. Within six months of the issue of these shares, their value had more than doubled, from 200p to 430p.

Like some of the other ITV companies, TVS has used non-network finance to diversify interests across a wide range of media operations. It has acquired a 62% holding in a Bristol-based company (Satellite

Technology Systems) which specialises in satellite television receivers. It has also bought an American film and television distributor (the Gilson Corporation), a group of British companies who stage media events (Button Design Contracts), and the Midem Organisation, the world's leading international media festival owner. Although its recent bid to acquire a share in the newly privatised French commercial television station TF1 was unsuccessful, TVS is still striving to fulfil its Chief Executive's 'strategic plan of a global entertainment servicing group'.

The Group Structure

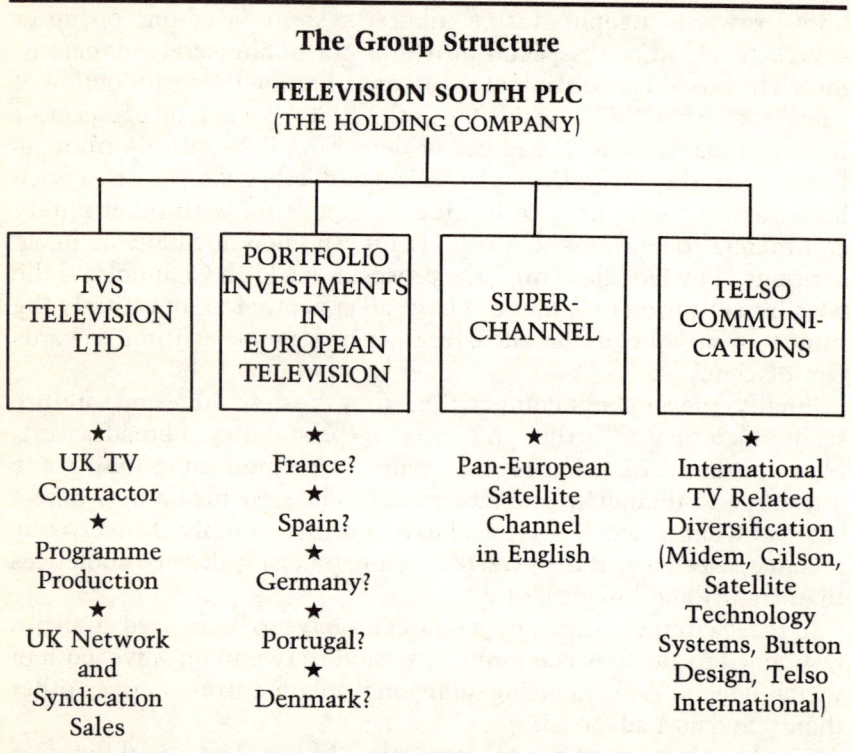

TELEVISION SOUTH PLC
(THE HOLDING COMPANY)

TVS TELEVISION LTD	PORTFOLIO INVESTMENTS IN EUROPEAN TELEVISION	SUPER-CHANNEL	TELSO COMMUNI-CATIONS
★ UK TV Contractor ★ Programme Production ★ UK Network and Syndication Sales	★ France? ★ Spain? ★ Germany? ★ Portugal? ★ Denmark?	★ Pan-European Satellite Channel in English	★ International TV Related Diversification (Midem, Gilson, Satellite Technology Systems, Button Design, Telso International)

Secondly, like several other companies, TVS has increased its sales of programmes to the overseas market (mainly in America). James Gatward, TVS' Chief Executive, spoke in 1986 of an 'aggressive growth in our programme supply for consumption locally on the UK network and abroad'. TVS' Chairman, Lord Boston, also acknowledged a 'dramatic acceleration in our film-making for the overseas market'. In fact, in the three years to October 1987, revenue from programme sales overall nearly trebled, to over £20m. Revenue from overseas sales increased tenfold to nearly £9m.

Gross Value of ITV Overseas Sales and Co-productions 1980–85
(Based on official IBA figures)

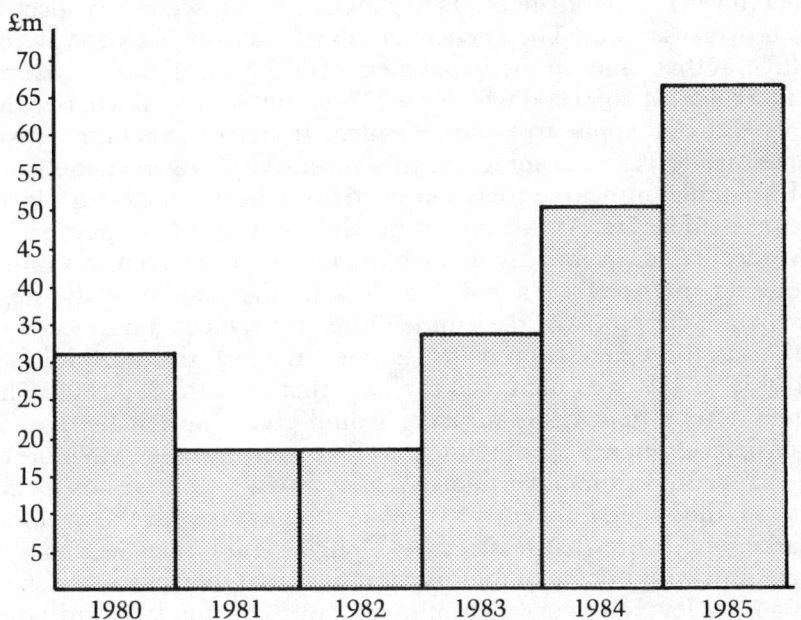

It should be emphasised that the way money is earned and spent by ITV companies is very complex. The economics of the industry are based, on the one hand, on relatively constant market forces. For example, the reliance on advertising income by ITV as a whole has been fairly stable in the last decade between 95% and 98% of total revenue. On the other hand, there are external pressures which increasingly threaten to destabilise the industry, like the threat of introducing advertisements on the BBC or of open competition for ITV franchises. Whatever the particular circumstances, financial strategies need to be finely tuned to prevailing market conditions.

What is more, these strategies have, by definition, to be prepared in advance of new circumstances arising. There is also the problem that large resources often have to be committed well ahead of the completion of a programme. There is no direct relationship, therefore, between the selling of air-time to advertisers and budgeting for programme production. Nevertheless, it is worth examining some of the system's more intricate financial features in a little more detail.

During the financial year which ended in October 1985, there was a clear incentive for broadcasters to generate useful secondary income from overseas sales. The Exchequer Levy (determined by the Home Office) at that time required a payment of 66.7% on all profits beyond a 'first slice' of £650,000 which the ITV companies retained. But the Levy did not apply to overseas sales. It made economic sense, therefore, to take advantage of this incentive. TVS' revenue from sales of programmes overseas increased from the previous year's level of £0.8m to £6.2m. At the same time, the amount of Levy payable by TVS decreased (in roughly inverse proportion) from £6m to £1.4m. However, in April 1986 (more or less in the middle of the next financial year for TVS) the Home Office introduced a new Levy of 22% on all revenue from overseas sales, reduced the standard rate payable to 45% and increased the free 'first slice' to £800,000. The Home Office hoped this measure would give a new incentive for industrial efficiency by allowing the ITV companies to retain more of their revenues from advertising. Whilst a new incentive was being offered, the original incentive to make programmes for the overseas market was somewhat reduced. As Douglas Hurd, then Secretary of State, put it. 'In order to preserve an incentive to exports, we shall propose a levy on overseas profits of about half the standard rate.' There was one obvious consequence of this for TVS. The changes in the rules on overseas earnings meant a virtual stagnation in overseas sales. As James Gatward commented, 'The uncertainty caused by the length of time taken to establish the new Exchequer Levy rate disrupted the pre-sale pattern of that particular type of expensive product . . . for foreign buyers'.

It might be expected that the amount of Levy payable would actually decrease as a result of the change in rate. But the situation was further complicated by the fact that advertising revenue throughout the network increased dramatically and beyond expectation (up 20%) during the year and even more so at TVS (up 25%). This meant that the amount of Levy payable also increased, in spite of the new lower rate introduced from April 1986. The Levy paid by TVS for the year ending in October 1986 rose by over 750% to £8.9m. However, if this spectacular rise is seen as a proportion of turnover and set against TVS' performance over a long period, then the 1986 Levy payment is not out of place; it is the level for 1985 which looks rather unusual. What is clear above all is that financial strategies are often complex. They are subject to distortion by changing fiscal environments and by time-frames which sometimes do not match the scale of the company's own operations.

Exchequer Levy Paid by TVS as a Percentage of Trading Profit

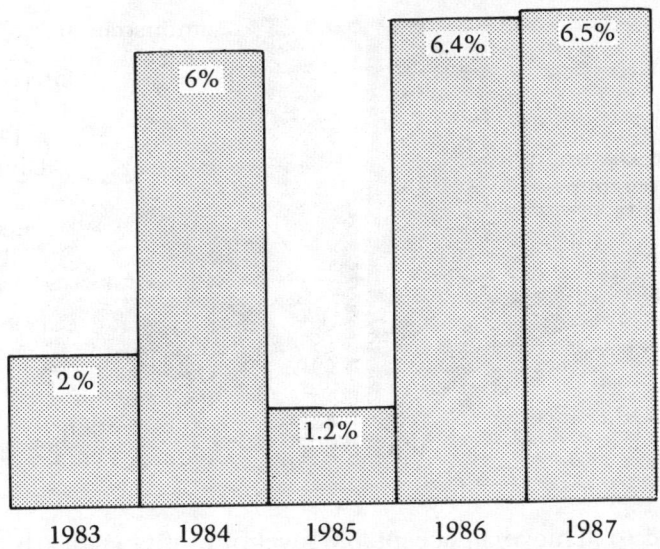

Good financial management demands a worthwhile return for investors. Thus, TVS has managed a steady increase in profitability in its first few years of operation, in spite of being a new company, and in spite of unpredictable financial factors. Since the first pay-out to shareholders in 1983, dividend per share has increased by more than 600%. In the financial year to October 1987, pre-tax profits increased by over 51%. TVS has become one of the most financially successful ITV companies in operation. With about 11% of the network's £1 billion turnover, TVS is in revenue terms the fifth largest ITV contractor.

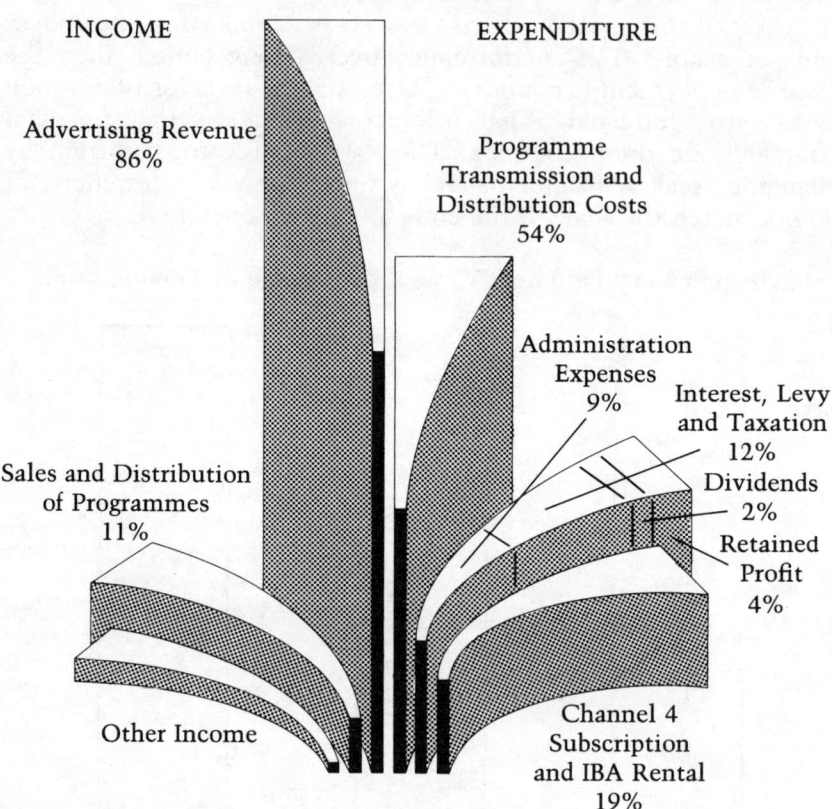

TVS Income Sources and Expenditure

INCOME

EXPENDITURE

Advertising Revenue
86%

Programme
Transmission and
Distribution Costs
54%

Administration
Expenses
9%

Interest, Levy
and Taxation
12%

Sales and Distribution
of Programmes
11%

Dividends
2%

Retained
Profit
4%

Other Income

Channel 4
Subscription
and IBA Rental
19%

The need to achieve an acceptable level of profits is clearly a vital matter for any ITV company. Maintaining or increasing profitability demands skill, knowledge and foresight. But it is, as this brief analysis of just one of many variables has suggested, a complex and uncertain operation. This means it is extremely difficult to generalise about the relationships between revenue, expenditure and output. The situation is further complicated by the diversity of TVS' media-related financial interests. As a result, it is very dangerous to make the kind of simplistic assumptions about the links between advertising and programmes which are often made. If there is no direct link between advertising revenue and programme production, what are the actual relationships between them?

Profit as a Proportion of Turnover at TVS (1983–87)

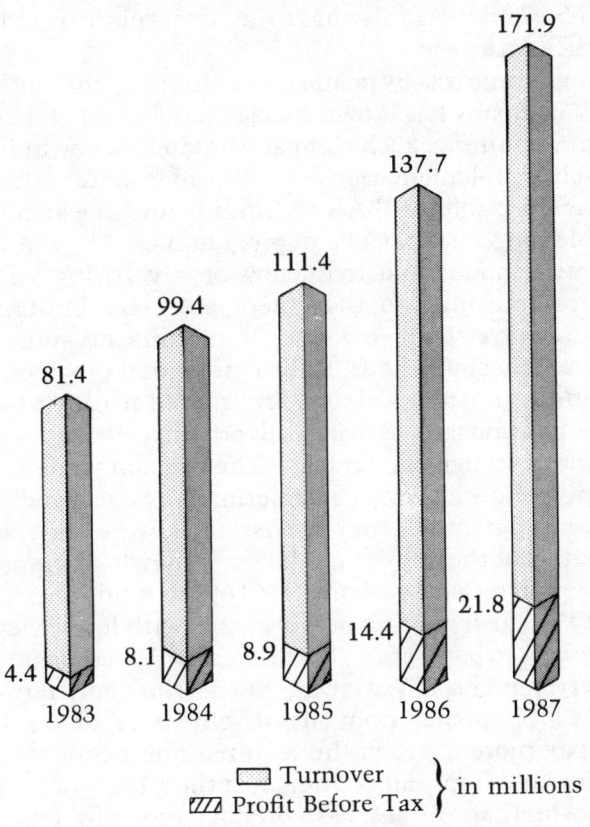

TVS Annual Report 1987

Programmes, audiences and advertising

If advertising revenue is to be maximised, those programmes which will attract enough viewers to encourage commercial clients to spend money on advertising their products and services are more likely to be transmitted. This necessarily means that certain kinds of programme are made with a broad appeal, and are then broadcast at specific points in the daily television schedules when most viewers are expected to be watching. From a purely commercial point of view, the ideal programme is the one which costs least to transmit but attracts most viewers and therefore advertising revenue. Hence the popularity in television schedules of recycled American 'soaps' like *Dallas. The Real World* also has to justify its place in part by reference to audience ratings.

But programming is by no means as simple as this outline suggests. Each ITV company has it own specialities, but all of them depend on *mixed programming*. Each company produces a portfolio of programmes which complement each other and offer some variety. The terms of the franchise and the IBA's continuing role as watchdog demand a reasonable range and balance of programmes. The IBA also controls the overall amount and frequency of advertising which the ITV companies transmit, so that there are clear limitations on the increase of advertising revenue. It permits no more than seven minutes in any single hour. Half-hour factual programmes like *The Real World* are not allowed to be interrupted at all by advertisements.

So the relationship between advertising, programmes and audiences is not a straightforward one. The ITV companies cannot and do not simply follow a policy of attracting the largest audience possible for every programme they transmit. In the case of TVS, the complexities of the system produce a somewhat surprising paradox. It has a very large share (about 11%) of the total advertising revenue earned by television. But it achieves this with lower viewing figures, proportionate to population, than several other companies. Its ratings are lower than the ITV average, yet in the short term, it actually generates more money from advertisements. As a result advertisers need to pay more to reach the required number of viewers.

This does not imply any criticism of the quality of its programmes, most of which are in any case produced for the network by other companies. The lower viewing figures are a result of the life-styles and television viewing habits of the TVS region's population, which are only partially dependent on the actual programmes shown.

TVS has, in fact, about the same *share* of total television viewing as London. If it did not, it would come under other financial pressures from advertisers. Persistently low ratings would put downward pressure on the price of advertising, even where demand for air-time exceeds supply. In the context of competition from cable and satellite channels, low ratings would be damaging to any ITV company.

The Southern companies dominate the ITV network in a way which is disproportionate to their viewing populations. The key to the ratings and advertising revenue paradox is that this North-South division corresponds with the distribution of wealth. There is a higher proportion of A, B and C1 social class viewers in the South, and these viewers are not only wealthier but also watch less television in general, and ITV in particular, than those further North. It follows that in order for an advertisement to achieve the desired amount of exposure (viewings per person and total reach) in the South, it has to be shown more often there than elsewhere. The cost to the advertiser is therefore greater. One estimate puts the average cost as much as 50% higher on TVS than in some other regions. The cost is justified by the probability that higher levels of disposable income will result in more consumer purchases. Since advertisers eventually calculate the cost per thousand viewers reached, more money is ultimately spent on advertising in the South. If cultural or demographic change caused more viewers to watch, then advertisers would be able to reach more people for the same money, or the same number of people for less. But the system is not under the control of either advertisers or television companies, and much of their effort is necessarily unpredictable.

Socio-economic Profiles of ITV Audiences

	TVS (%)	Network (%)
AB	21	16
C1	24	21
C2	25	25
D	15	19
E	15	19
Total	100	100

BARB/AGB Establishment Survey March 1986

TVS transmits to 9.4% of UK adults but to 11.4% of A, B, C1 adults

In spite of the complexity and unpredictability of the system, advertising revenue is a vitally important factor in any ITV company's success or survival. There is clearly a general link between the kind of programmes shown and the kind of advertising revenue they generate, but the precise relationship is complicated. Is it the

case that rather than advertising determining programmes, programmes determine advertising? If this were the case, then we would
expect a close correspondence between the audiences who actually
watch a particular programme and the consumers of the particular
goods and services advertised around the programme. This sort of
relationship is clearly implied by some of the advertisements carried
by Channel 4's American football programme, for example.

The Real World audience

So who does watch *The Real World?* The simple answer is that
nobody really seems to know. The ratings figures from the Broadcasters' Audience Research Board are based on sampling techniques
which estimate the number of viewers watching at a given time (the
gross viewing figures). They also calculate the percentage of the total
television audience watching at a given time (the TVR) and the total
audience share for each channel. In addition, the Appreciation Index
offers some qualitative information about responses to particular
programmes (the AI). Direct responses come from viewers in the form
of telephone calls, letters and requests for 'back-up' material. There is
also occasionally some qualitative research done with viewing
groups by IBA, ITV and BBC research departments.

All of these indices are informative in their own way but require
careful interpretation. They are certainly of some value to *The Real
World* team in forming an 'inside' view of who their audience is. But
this view is by no means uniform and often seems to be based on a
variety of hunches. Some of the team have no idea at all; others claim
an audience with a majority of males who reflect the programme's
technological bias. One view is that it is a programme 'for all the
family' which children, parents and grandparents can understand – a
view supported by the letters and drawings from children received in
the mail-bag. Another view is of an audience comprising two main
groups: the under 30s, who need a fast-moving brief on science and
technology; and the over 45s, who may feel threatened by the pace of
change and find the programme's friendly style makes technology
less intimidating.

The advertisements also give some indication of who is expected to
be watching at the scheduled time. There is an increasing tendency
within broadcasting to segment television audiences and position
them more precisely in relation to particular product advertisements.

Individual advertisements can now be correlated with particular age, gender or social groups. What kind of viewers might be expected to be watching at 7pm on a Monday evening? What clues do the advertisements give?

Advertisements Around *Dead as the Dodo?* in the TVS Region

6.56pm	10/6/85	
Spot	Product Name	Length
01	Nescafe	030
02	Walkers Crisps	030
03	Bird's Eye Steak-house Grills	030
04	Delikat	030
05	Elmlea Cream Substitute	030
06	Optrex Lotion and Drops	020
07	AA Membership	020
08	Poole Holiday Guide	010
09	PO National Giro	020
10	Zanussi Washing Machine	010
7.26pm		
01	Halifax Building Society	030
02	PO Datapost	030
03	Konica Films	030
04	KP Crunchie Waffles	020
05	Vitbe High Bran	010

If we look at the figures for *The Real World* series of 1985 as a whole, we find that it averaged about 7.3 million viewers. This is comparable with similar series transmitted at 7pm in the same season in other years. Given the unusual socio-economic profile of the TVS region, it is perhaps surprising that the biggest single audience group consisted of what the industry calls 'the old and downmarket'. It is less surprising when we recall that the programme is 'hammocked' between *Crossroads* and *Coronation Street* and therefore shares many viewers with these other popular programmes. As Garfield Kennedy says, 'we do benefit from people watching *Crossroads* and they still sit there staring at the box'. Even so, compared with the

A view across the schedules, Monday June 10th 1985

BBC 1	BBC 2	ITV/TVS	C4
6.00 The Six O'Clock News	6.00 Film: The Birth of the Blues	6.00 Coast to Coast	6.00 The Old Country
6.35 Regional Magazine		6.40 Airmail	6.30 The Art of Persuasion
7.00 Wogan	7.25 Flower of the Month	7.00 **The Real World**	7.00 Channel 4 News
7.40 Fame	7.35 Fat Man in the Kitchen	7.30 Coronation St	
8.25 'Allo 'Allo	8.05 The Living Planet	8.00 Des O'Connor Now!	8.00 Brookside
		8.30 World in Action	8.30 Man About the House
9.00 The Nine O'Clock News	9.00 The Young Ones	9.00 Jenny's War	9.00 End of Empire
9.25 Panorama	9.35 The Paul Daniels Magic Show		
10.05 Film: Bob and Carol and Ted and Alice	10.15 Ravi Shankar	10.00 News at Ten	10.00 Murder in a Mist
	10.55 Newsnight	10.30 Kojak	10.35 The Eleventh Hour
		11.30 The Protectors	
11.50 Weather	11.40 Weather	12.00 Jazz Special	12.15 Close
11.55 Close	11.50 Close	12.30 Closedown	

programme's national audiences, the TVS region consistently provides a higher proportion of social class A, B and C1 viewers.

For *Dead as the Dodo?* On June 10th 1985, nearly half of the audience in the TVS region were over 55 years old. Over half of the audience were female and less than a third of the audience were from social class A, B, or C1. The figures were not significantly different for the other programmes in the series. But they are different from, for example, *Tomorrow's World*. The BBC programme has a very similar gross viewing figure and transmission time, but takes its largest single viewing group in the TVS region from the 35–44 age-range.

These differences depend only partly on the style and content of the programmes, but much more on what other programmes are scheduled around them and against them. Simply shifting the transmission time of the 1986 series of *The Real World* to 9.50pm on Sundays meant that its audience changed significantly. The *size* of audience was reduced by about 2 million. But its *composition* also changed. The number of social class A, B and C1 viewers increased

The Real World: Audience Profiles by Social Class

Average % share Monday 7pm (3 June – 15 July 1985)		Average % share Sunday 9.50pm (6 July – 24 August 1986)	
NETWORK		NETWORK	
ABC1	25	ABC1	32
C2	35	C2	30
DE	40	DE	38
TVS REGION		TVS REGION	
ABC1	28	ABC1	44
C2	34	C2	32
DE	39	DE	25

both nationally and in the TVS region. The increase in 'up-market' viewers in the TVS region was particularly sharp.

One thing is very clear. The profile of the viewing audience which the figures suggest is not compatible with the view that the programmes determine the advertisements. Whatever criteria we use for establishing who watches *The Real World*, the programme itself does not determine the kind of advertising which surrounds it. We cannot, therefore, explain its identity simply in terms of its power to attract certain kinds of advertisements.

It is equally clear that the relationship does not work in reverse. The identity of *The Real World* is not determined by the advertisements which it carries. Advertising revenue is a necessary but not sufficient explanation of why *The Real World* is like it is. Advertising is clearly vital to the long-term viability of TVS and the ITV system as a whole. But it does not immediately determine the shape of the programmes which carry the advertisements.

Nor is advertising the only major factor which is vital to long-term viability, as Southern TV discovered to its cost when it lost the franchise to TVS. It is also important to maintain the satisfaction of its viewers and the confidence of the IBA. Here, perhaps, we can find a more complete explanation of why *The Real World* is like it is.

If the relationship between advertising and programmes is not accidental and if neither is simply and directly responsible for the other, there must be some other explanation. The question 'Why is *The Real World* like it is?' perhaps needs to be reformulated as 'Why is *The Real World* shown when it is?'

8

The Hidden Hand-Shake

The ITV network
The role of the IBA
The 'inside' view
A slot in the schedules

In order to establish why *The Real World* is like it is, we may also have to ask the more basic question: why is *The Real World* produced at all? The answer to this is by no means as obvious as it might seem. It involves asking some supplementary questions as well. Why is *The Real World* networked? Why does it appear at a particular time in the schedules?

There is something apparently natural about the times at which particular programmes occur. In fact, planning the schedules is a highly skilled and complex art carried out by specialists whose work is subject both to the demands of the IBA and the viewing habits of television audiences.

This chapter explores how the identity of *The Real World* relates to its position in the schedules. It also suggests how the politics of the ITV system have allowed *The Real World* its particular niche in the network.

The ITV network

In one sense TVS operates as a completely independent company. It sells advertising space around its programmes both on ITV and Channel 4 to clients within and beyond its own region. But it does not actually operate alone. It does not produce all its own programmes or

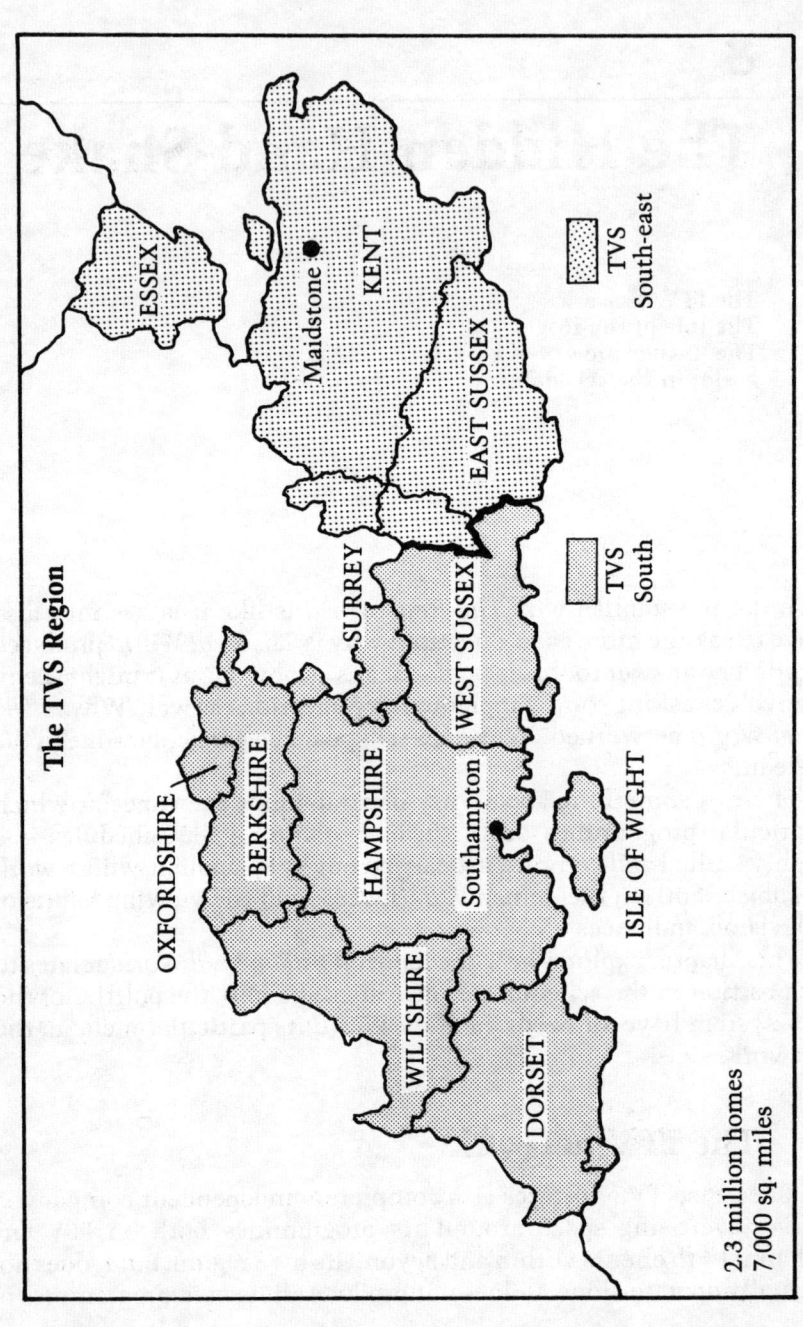

The TVS Region

ESSEX

KENT

Maidstone ●

EAST SUSSEX

SURREY

WEST SUSSEX

OXFORDSHIRE

BERKSHIRE

HAMPSHIRE

Southampton ●

ISLE OF WIGHT

WILTSHIRE

DORSET

TVS
South-east

TVS
South

2.3 million homes
7,000 sq. miles

have complete freedom to show what it wants when it wants to. It is part of a complex federal system. The BBC, by contrast, has a fairly monolithic structure. Its five English regions and three other national regions are responsible to the central hierarchy. Although this leads to some tensions between regional and metropolitan interests, it is a fairly stable and well co-ordinated system.

BBC English Broadcasting Regions (1986–)

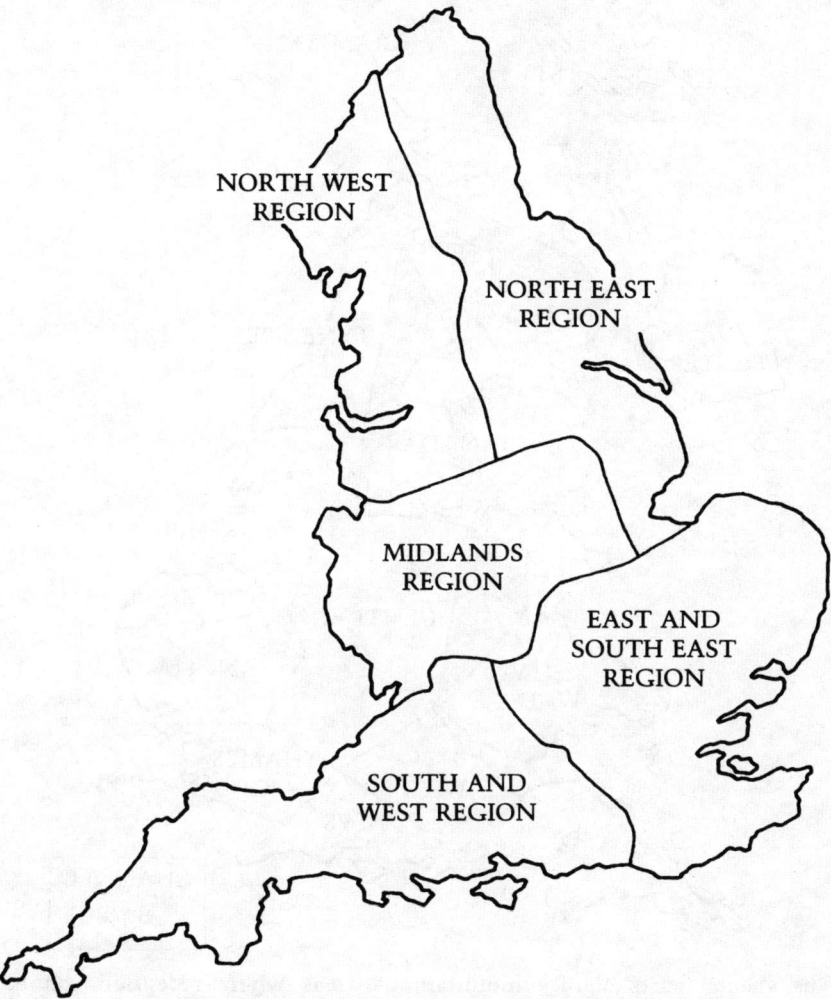

The ITV Regions

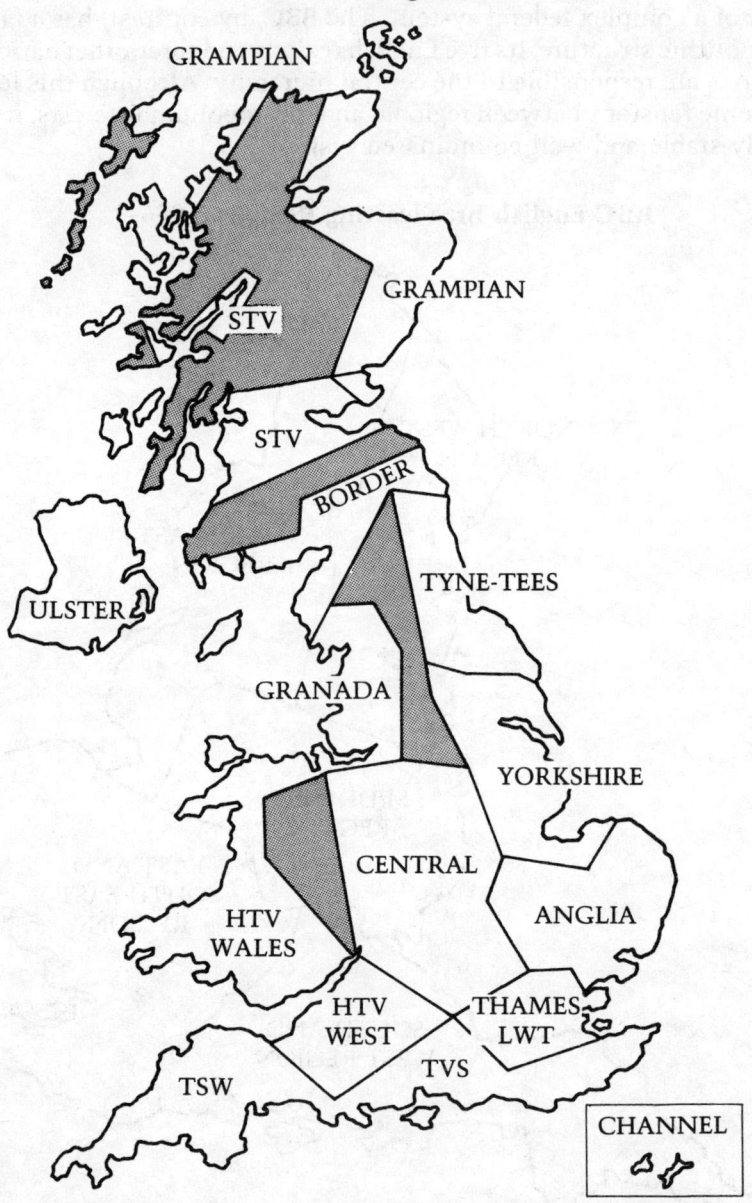

(The shaded parts signify mountainous areas where reception can be difficult)

The way the ITV system works is described by Chris Dunkley as follows:

> Theoretically each of the fifteen programme companies retains complete autonomy and may show whatever programmes it likes in its own region, provided it complies with the IBA's mandates and requirements on current affairs and so on. In practice most of the national network shows the same programmes most of the time, but the means by which this uniformity is achieved are described even by those who manage it as Byzantine in their complexity
>
> (Dunkley, 1985, p. 54).

As with the other ITV companies, the terms of TVS' franchise allow for the production of both local and nationally networked programmes. (A networked programme is shown by all the other ITV companies. A regional programme is shown only within a particular company's own area.) In 1986, TVS was asked to produce a weekly average of at least 11½ hours of new local interest material. In the event, it produced slightly more than was required. Its original programme output in 1986–7 amounted to 780 hours, 25% of which were networked (including Channel 4 and part-networked programmes).

The relationships between the different ITV companies are complex and still evolving. But the major developments since the creation of ITV were neatly summarised by the IBA when it looked back over its first twenty-one years:

> From the beginning the Independent Television system has been plural and regional. The first Television Act of 1954 required the Authority to do all it could to ensure adequate competition to supply programmes between a number of separate programme companies. The Act also said that in the programmes transmitted from any station there should be a 'suitable proportion of matter calculated to appeal specially to the tastes and outlook of persons served by the station or stations'.
>
> Television production is costly. Large resources in finance, technical apparatus and skilled specialised manpower are needed to sustain a regular weekly output of important productions in light entertainment, drama or current affairs. The Authority considered that the task of producing such programmes should fall mainly on the

The Structure of Independent Television in Britain (1983–)

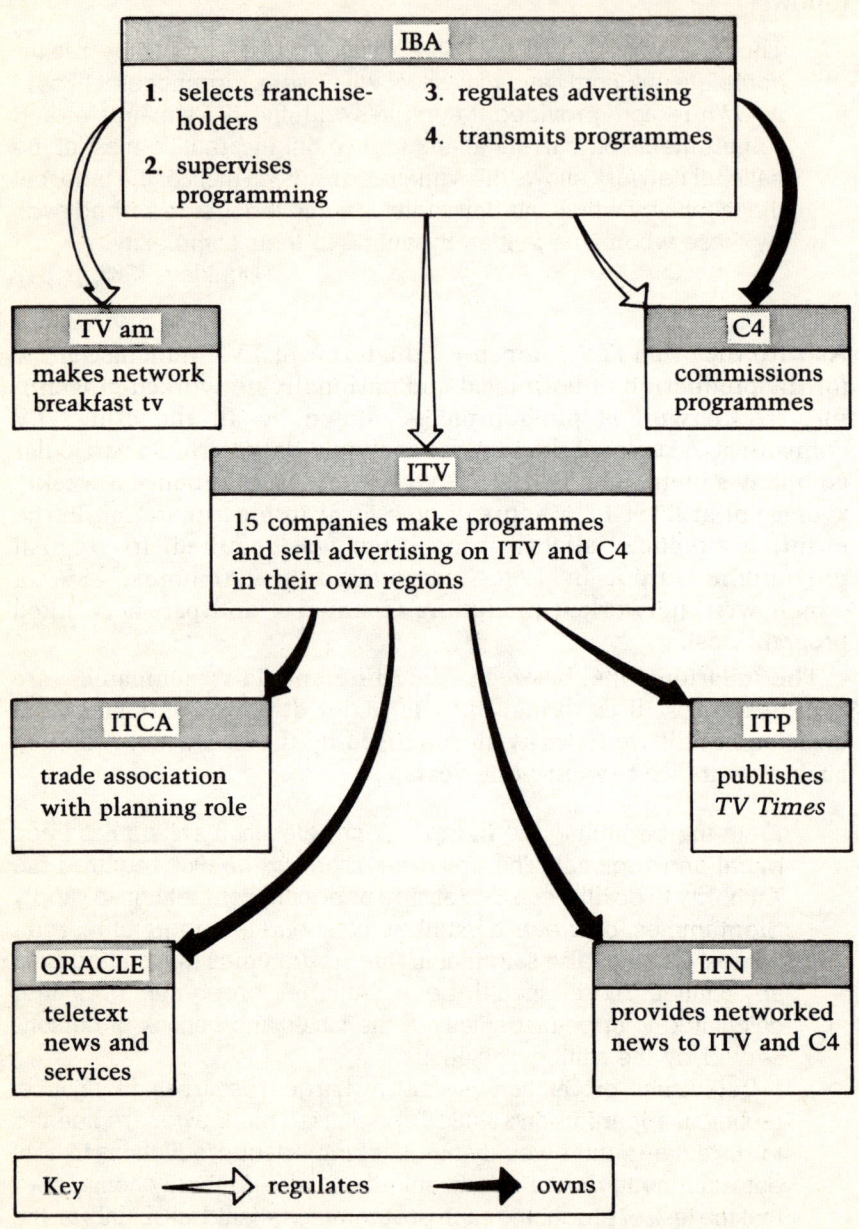

IBA

1. selects franchise-holders
2. supervises programming
3. regulates advertising
4. transmits programmes

TV am

makes network breakfast tv

C4

commissions programmes

ITV

15 companies make programmes and sell advertising on ITV and C4 in their own regions

ITCA

trade association with planning role

ITP

publishes *TV Times*

ORACLE

teletext news and services

ITN

provides networked news to ITV and C4

Key ⟹ regulates ➤ owns

largest companies which could expect a higher revenue from the areas they served. The Authority therefore created a system made up of several large so-called 'network companies' and a number of smaller 'regional companies'. In the main, the network companies make the programmes that are seen in the whole country; the first task of the regional companies is held to be production for their own areas. From 1955–68 there were four major or network companies; since 1968 there have been five, providing a central core of programmes for the whole country, that is, both for themselves and for the ten regional companies.

The five largest companies – Thames, London Weekend, ATV, Granada and Yorkshire – are the main providers of network programmes to be used by the whole service. They need considerable staff and resources if they are systematically to provide a reliable, steady and complete supply of programmes of sufficiently high standard. The areas served by these companies are planned to be large enough to give them the income needed to carry out this task. Three of the network companies are based not in London but at television centres in the most heavily populated regions of the country. So Independent Television has established main centres for the production of national programmes also at Manchester, Leeds, and Birmingham.

The primary reason for the existence of the ten regional companies is for the provision of truly local programme services. But the local companies make many other contributions to the Independent Television system as a whole. Local programme initiatives have frequently led to the adoption of programme ideas by other companies, and important contributions to the development of news magazines, adult education, school and religious programmes have stemmed from the regional companies. A number of children's documentary and drama programmes seen throughout the country are produced by the larger regional companies, and all the companies from time to time produce programmes which are presented in several areas or nationally. Arrangements exist for the regular scrutiny of available programmes from the regions, and such programmes are in network distribution every week of the year.

The removal in 1972 of the Government's restrictions on the hours of broadcasting gave an opportunity to extend the full or partial networking of regional programmes.

(*Television and Radio*, 1987, p. 10).

The ITV Companies

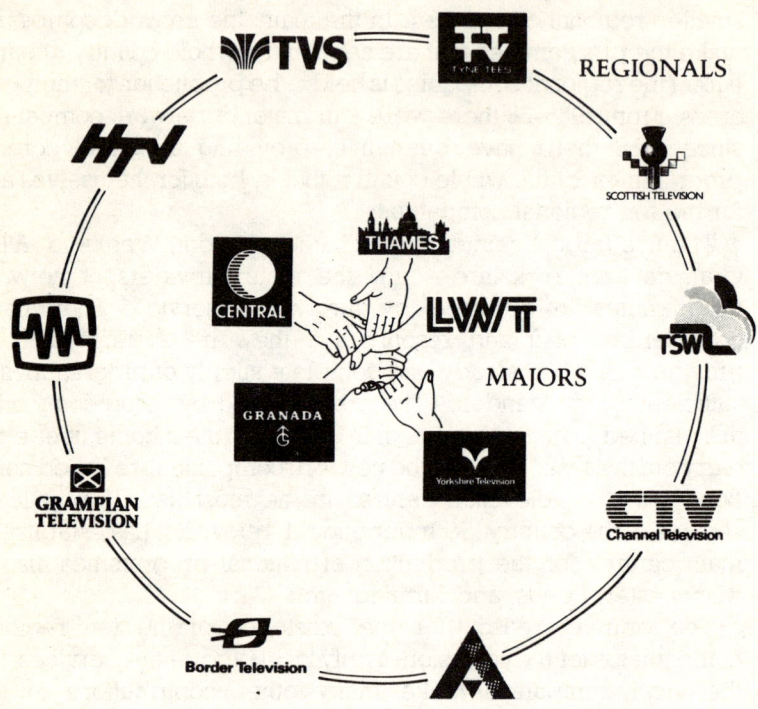

NB: TV am and ITN are separate companies based in London

There have been many changes since 1972. ATV has been replaced by Central, TSW has replaced Westward and TVS has superseded Southern. Average weekly programme output from the ITV network has risen by about 50% to 105 hours, which has meant new obligations for the Majors and new opportunities for the Regionals. But it remains the case that the Majors have the largest share (60%) of total advertising revenue.

In addition to its own programmes, each ITV company transmits programmes made by the other companies. But this is by no means an equal exchange. The main traffic involves the Regionals (including

TVS) buying programmes from the Majors. The historical development of ITV has produced a situation where the regional companies have to pay for the standard programmes made by the Majors even if they do not transmit them. They do so because

- they could not afford to make such programmes themselves
- the Majors' programmes have usually delivered larger audiences
- they are obliged to by the 'Live Network Agreement'.

The so-called 'Live Network Agreement' relies on the creation of a pool of programmes known as 'Category A' material which the Majors sell to the Regionals. This pool forms a guarantee to the regional companies of a known number of hours of material each year (currently about 2,000 hours at a total cost of around £60m). The Regionals pay at an agreed rate based on the previous year's percentage of total Network Advertising Revenue (NAR). As a result TVS, with the largest share of NAR (about 11%) amongst the ten regional companies, pays the most for 'Category A' material produced by the Majors (currently more than a quarter of the total bill). The Majors also produce other material ('Category B') which is offered to the rest of the network on an optional basis and at an agreed discounted rate which is independent of NAR.

The amount of material which each of the Majors is expected to produce every year is also determined by its share of NAR. The greater the percentage share, the greater the obligation to make programmes for the network. They also exchange programmes amongst themselves according to a tariff system of their own making. This establishes points for different categories of programmes and the total number of points available is determined annually as a basis for calculating each Major's contribution. It is essentially a barter system operated by the Majors' Programme Controllers which involves no financial exchanges between them. It has occasionally led to complaints from the Regionals that they are being treated unfairly, since, they claim, the Majors are effectively able to discount each others' wares whilst maintaining the 'cover-price' to the Regionals. In response, the Majors argue that the long-term obligation to produce network programmes is costly since they recover only about 25% of their production costs from the Regionals whilst allowing the Regionals a greater proportion of costs on specific kinds of programme.

The Programme Controller's Group (NCG) is also responsible for the precise details of the ITV schedule. It consists of the Programme Controllers (or Directors of Programmes) of the major companies, the IBA's Director of Television and the Director of the Network Programme Planning Secretariat from the Independent Television Association (ITVA), which represents all fifteen companies. Since 1987, two Directors of Programmes (including one from TVS) from the Regional companies have been added to the NCG. It meets weekly with a view to producing outline schedules covering a three month block of future programming. These outlines are then put to all the programme-making companies as a basis for building up their own schedules.

They are not necessarily accepted in their entirety but negotiated in the light of regional requirements and the kind of financial constraints already considered. Two or three months ahead of transmission, each company submits its detailed schedule for approval by the IBA, according to established criteria and quotas for the balance and timing of particular kinds of programme.

This may suggest that there is unanimity amongst the Majors. But there are real differences of interest and viewpoint between them. Nor is the situation a static one. Over the last fifteen years, there has been a continual increase in the amount of material made by the regional companies for network transmission. This has happened for a variety of reasons such as spare production capacity and an increased need for UK domestic programmes which the Majors are unwilling or unable to produce. Even over the last decade, there has been a small but clear shift in the proportion of home-produced networked material which comes from the regional companies.

Getting programmes networked is much more difficult, however, for the Regionals than for the Majors, since they have no guaranteed access to the ITV schedule. Each proposal has to go through a complex system administered by the ITVA. Pilots are often requested before a series can go into production and, as with all ITV programmes, it is unlikely that transmission details will be known even when production has begun.

The level of payment which the Regionals receive for their programmes from the network when they do manage to achieve transmission is decided by negotiation between the PCG (mainly representing the Majors) and the regional company. The basic principle is that Regionals can recover a portion of their indirect costs and their allowable direct costs as agreed by the current ITVA

Share of Network Production 1976–7

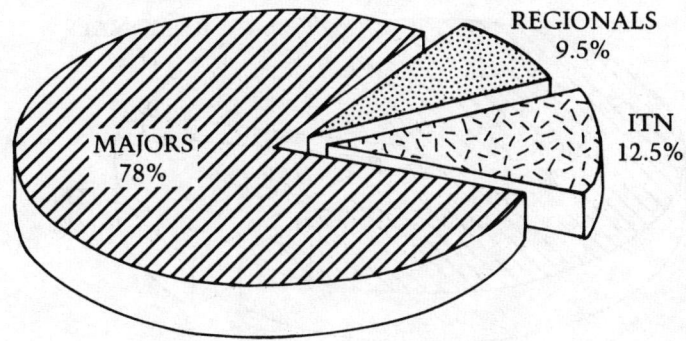

IBA Annual Report and Accounts 1976–77

rate-card, which determines a common framework for all the regional companies. There is, however, a ceiling imposed on the total figure recoverable. This is known as the Maximum Hourly Rate (MHR) and Regionals cannot price their programmes above this level. Once a price is agreed which conforms to these principles, charges are made on transmission in accordance with NAR share.

The whole system is currently being re-assessed by the ITV companies, by the IBA and by the Government, since there is a growing recognition of the 'Catch 22' whereby, in order to have their programmes networked, smaller companies have to do more with less money. They have to convince the Majors of the quality and value of their programmes but on the basis of a financial handicap. The major ITV companies are still responsible for the majority of networked programmes, in spite of developments since the early 1970s. In 1986, the Big Five networked more than four times as many programmes as the other ten companies.

David Mellor, former Minister of State at the Home Office, indicated the Government's desire for change: 'We are looking to produce a new framework of legislation for broadcasting and it is one of our key thoughts at the moment as to whether it should contain the ability to change the networking arrangement.'

As Chris Dunkley describes it, it is a system based on 'the manipulation of a tangled web of motives: prestige, profit, revenge,

Share of Network Production 1985–6

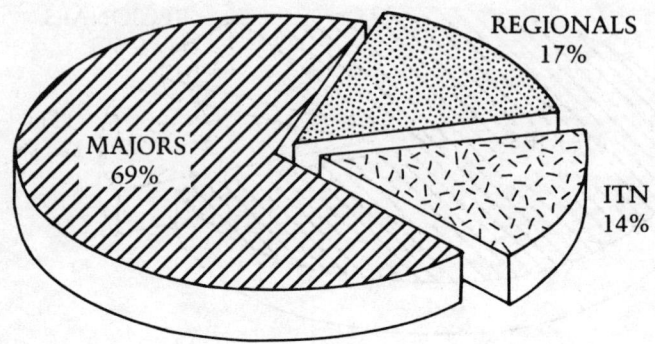

Television and Radio 1987

but above all the need to co-operate enough to maintain the system and hold off the common opponent' (Dunkley, 1985, p. 54).

The role of the IBA

The IBA can and does exert an influence not only on schedules but on the balance of programmes which come from the Regionals and the Majors. Even so, beyond carrying out its legal duty to ensure that its codes of practice and scheduling rules are observed, it can do little; it must persuade, cajole and support wherever it can. It remains dependent on the major companies in negotiating changes to the schedule. The general codes of practice which the IBA publishes from time to time concentrate on explaining what programme makers need to avoid rather than on positive standards for programmes. The content, style and values of particular programmes remain very much the preserve of the producing companies. A somewhat cynical view is put by Nicholas Garnham: 'The interlocking of programme commitments is such that, like a house of cards, pull one out and the lot come down . . . The result is that it mandates a few prestige programmes and leaves the major part of peak-time viewing to the grossest commercial pressures' (Garnham, 1980, p. 25). It is likely that dissatisfaction with it will result in a revised system of financial exchange in the future. The question of access to network time remains, in the meantime, a difficult and contentious issue.

Programme Transmission on ITV* (Weekly average 1985–6)

	Duration Hrs. Mins	Percentage %
News and news magazines	11:01	10.50
Current affairs and general factual	10:54	10.25
Arts	0:42	0.75
Religion	2:31	2.50
Adult education	1:51†	1.75
School programmes	6:50	6.50
Pre-school	3:35	3.50
Children's informative programmes	2:12	2
INFORMATIVE	39:36	37.75
Plays, series, TV movies	26:21	25
Feature films	8:18	8
NARRATIVE	34:39	33
Children's drama and entertainment	7:24	7
Entertainment and light music	14:29	13.75
Sport	9:00	8.50
TOTAL ALL PROGRAMMES	105:15††	100

Excluding TV-am's 21 hours per week.
†To this total should be added 13 minutes per week of general factual material shown at peak-time which was accepted by the IBA as educationally valuable and supported by educational material and activities.
††Opening captions totalling 7 minutes per week are not specified above, but are included in the total.

Television and Radio 1987

Under the terms of a standing agreement with the NCG, the IBA protects some of ITV's adult educational material, which might be perceived as 'vulnerable' during peak viewing-time, by earmarking it for special treatment. A small amount of general factual material (26 programmes totalling 13 hours each year) is designated as 'Serious In Peak Recommended for Inclusion in Quota' (SIP/RIQ). The companies who produce such programmes also support them with supplementary resources because of their educational value. *The*

Real World was first included in this specially privileged category for networked transmission in 1983. But it lost this special status in 1986.

It is certainly to TVS' advantage for *The Real World* to be networked. In addition to the payments they receive from the network which they would not receive for a regional programme (about half of the relevant costs), they also avoid paying for another programme which they would otherwise have bought from elsewhere in the network. There is, as well, a certain amount of kudos for the individuals involved in the programme team if their material is networked. At the same time, and perhaps more significantly for TVS, it provides a measure of corporate prestige and a gentle reminder to the network about the capacity of a Regional to deliver the goods at network level. This could enhance its claims to Major status, not merely on the basis of its turnover and NAR, but also on the basis of its programme quality and audience ratings.

The ability to finance the making of a programme that can attract a large audience is only part of the problem. There is also the need for appropriate staff and skills to sustain the quality required of network programmes. There is currently no regular weekly slot on ITV for general science programmes like *The Real World*. As a result, no ITV company has the permanent staff and expertise to mount science programmes efficiently or effectively. The odds against success are stacked very high.

Is *The Real World*, then, no more than the result of network politics? Is it merely a tactical manoeuvre designed to further TVS' ambitions for Major status? Or is the agreement by the Majors to network it merely a casual offering of crumbs from under the table of the Big Five?

The 'inside' view

From TVS' point of view, *The Real World* is potentially a source of the 'programme strength' with which it is trying to persuade the IBA that it deserves Major status. In its formal submission to the IBA in September 1986, it argued that such a move was necessary not only for TVS' sake but was also a fundamental requirement for the future of the ITV system. It has achieved considerable success with certain kinds of programme which have achieved very high viewing figures nationally. It has almost trebled the amount of its programming which is networked since it began broadcasting in 1982. In 1987 it sold 26 hours of entertainment to the network; all of its children's output (over 80 hours) was networked; and there were several 'one-off' documentaries and some drama (e.g. *Mandela*) which also achieved high ratings.

Yet Greg Dyke (until 1987, TVS' Director of Programmes) has argued that it is 'uneconomic' for TVS to make high-ratings programmes for the network since TVS did not recover even the direct costs on programmes like *Bobby Davro*. Certainly, the basic anomalies of the current exchange system put the Regionals at a disadvantage when it comes to making network programmes, except on an occasional basis with certain kinds of programme.

By comparison with most programmes on the ITV network, *The Real World* is unusual. Its annual seven-week run and the need for its network status to be renegotiated every time its short season returns make it something of an oddity. Yet it is in many ways typical of the problems which a non-Major ITV company may experience when it tries to compete with the Majors. The scheduling of *The Real World* has in fact been at the centre of one of the most bitter rows within the network during the last decade, all of which has occurred behind closed doors.

Financial constraints certainly play their part in determining the identity of *The Real World*. Although accurate costs are difficult to calculate, the average cash and facilities cost per programme in 1986 was nearly £60,000. This may sound a great deal, but it is only about twice the cost of making a thirty second commercial or the gross revenue generated by the advertisements in one hour of peak-time viewing. Only about half of these costs are recovered in fixed payments from the network. On the other hand, some programmes do not even recover their direct costs. *The Real World* is unusual amongst TVS programmes in that it does at least recover its direct costs through network payments.

But there is no direct relationship between the programme budget and the amount of money raised by its surrounding advertisements. Selling air-time and making programmes are separate operations. Advertising revenue is actually dependent on the time-slot rather than the programme. Since some programmes are more expensive to make than others (e.g. drama), subsidy by cheaper programmes further complicates the relationship between budgets and revenues.

Nevertheless, *The Real World's* budget is certainly an important influence on its quality, since it directly determines the amount of filming, editing and studio time which it gets. Silverstone estimated the production costs of the *Horizon* programme he studied at £80,000. Since this programme involved seventeen weeks' filming compared with *The Real World's* three days, it makes the latter look rather extravagant. In reality, however, the BBC's and ITV's accounting procedures are completely different so no direct comparisons are possible.

The economics and politics of the ITV network are far more important factors, however, than individual programme budgets. The network clearly imposes hidden constraints on the kind of budget which is allocated to an occasional series like *The Real World*. In practice, this means that the lead-time for research must be restricted. Instead of developing over a considerable period of time, programmes tend to rely on material which fits best into a six month production cycle.

Not surprisingly, the 'inside' view is overwhelmingly that production expertise is the most important factor in determining *The Real World's* identity. This is certainly true in a very specific sense, and it is perhaps hard to imagine production staff saying anything else. There is, nevertheless, a clear majority view that the programme budget is the next most important factor. Equal third in importance according to the production team are the schedule time and audience.

Significantly, there is no mention of advertising revenue. Clearly, in the minds of the production staff, the programme works with relative independence from the company's main source of income. There is no real contradiction here, however. It is at the level of scheduling that the general dependence on advertising revenue operates.

A slot in the schedules

The particular slot in the schedule in which *The Real World* is transmitted defines both the audience and the advertisements the programme carries. In other words, if *The Real World* moved its schedule time the particular audience and advertisements would not move with it. Instead, it would acquire a substantially new audience and completely different advertisements, as appropriate to that new transmission time. (The changes in audience size and composition which occurred as a result of the actual schedule change in 1986 have already been discussed.)

There is a peculiar kind of momentum at work which helps

TV Times June 10th 1985/July 6th 1986

seasonal series like *The Real World* to keep returning to the network schedule. When Michael Blackstad began the series in 1982 after leaving the BBC and *Tomorrow's World*, *The Real World* was made an important part of TVS' franchise promises and of their youthful programming plans. After his departure from the company, the series continued on the enthusiasm of a handful of programme makers. It had the support of TVS management, the encouragement of the IBA and the indulgence of the Majors. It was able to fill an obvious gap in ITV provision for which there were few tenders.

What it lacked, however, was the stability and security which come from the confidence that the programme has a slot in the schedules which does not have to be negotiated and fought for on an annual basis. The continuing cycle of uncertainty which became a way of life for *The Real World* may explain a good deal of the programme's anxiety to please and its sometimes neurotic jokiness.

In its Mid-Term Review, the IBA specifically commended TVS for having 'strengthened the ITV science output with *The Real World*'. No doubt this was powerful encouragement for the production team and for the company, especially given the knowledge that franchises are not everlasting, as TVS' predecessors discovered. Given also TVS' declared ambition to achieve Major status, it is difficult to see how it could afford not to fight for the survival of the series. To abandon the fight would mean losing an opportunity to demonstrate its ability to make network programmes. It would also mean losing face with the Majors. This would make it even more difficult in future to persuade the Majors to take their programmes for networking.

However, the IBA's Review made several other comments about programming on a more general level: 'The company has undoubtedly enjoyed considerable success in expanding the business side of its operations and attaining high levels of profitability; but the same energy and purpose have not always been fully matched on the programme side where the record is uneven . . .' Such comments suggest that the pursuit of Major status will not be easy. On the face of it, the loss of the special SIP/RIQ slot on the ITV network may also indicate a need for caution in the battle for Major status. TVS has noted these criticisms and has taken steps to remedy the situation.

Officially *The Real World's* future is still under consideration, and it could theoretically be included in the portfolio of 'offers' which TVS regularly makes (along with the other Regionals) to the

NCG. But the slot which it once occupied has since been filled by other programmes and the programme team has dispersed.

Central's *The Cutting Edge* is an interesting successor as a science series. It manages to avoid some of the obvious pitfalls of popular science programmes and takes some unusual risks. In its own words, it is concerned with 'the daily lives of a wide variety of . . . scientists, as they struggle towards success . . . and failure'. Scheduled in the same SIP/RIQ slot at 7pm on Monday as *The Real World*, and against the same BBC1 competition (*Wogan*), *The Cutting Edge* has not gone so far afield but has concentrated instead on what is going on in Oxford. It also offers a different style of presentation from *The Real World*. Its visual rhythm is very similar, with an average shot length of 5 seconds, but its style is altogether more leisurely. Its use of location film is more lavish and it allows scientists to speak for themselves more frequently. These features place it more in the *Horizon* mould. Yet it has managed to achieve audiences as high as 7.3 million and has averaged 6.2 million over the first six programmes of the series in the Monday night slot, This is only slightly down on the directly comparable 1985 *The Real World* series' average of 7.3 million and substantially more than the Sunday night slot average of 5.3 million.

The demise of *The Real World* should not be seen, however, as a failure but should be set in the context of a new phase in TVS' struggle for Major status within the ITV system. Major status has become more important than the battle over network slots. If Major status were achieved, there would be no need for TVS to fight on such unequal terms for their own programmes. The battle may have been lost but the war is only just beginning.

The Real World has gone the same way as the dodo and the quagga, and it is unlikely that currently available cloning techniques will be able to revive it. But from its ashes and from the reconstruction of the ITV network may at least emerge a new variation on the established stock of science programmes, or even, perhaps, a completely new species.

9
Reactions and Responses

Press and public
Audience research
Programmes and viewers
Messages and meanings
Mapping responses
Creating a dialogue
Critical autonomy

Collecting and interpreting audience responses is a difficult and expensive process. The kind which is routinely collected through the BARB mechanism is rarely of much use to programme makers and sometimes discounted by them in favour of their own notions of audiences.

The 'inside' view of what shapes *The Real World* relegates audiences into third place after production expertise and programme budget. Some members of the production team have very clear views on who the programme is aimed at, but these views vary. There also appears to be some discrepancy between their ideas of who is assumed to be watching and who actually does.

This chapter discusses first of all the problems which science programmes have in addressing audiences and the kinds of feed-back available to broadcasters through the press and through their own research. Secondly, it discusses how particular audiences responded to *Dead as the Dodo?* in the context of current knowledge about how audiences respond to television. Finally, some suggestions and possible solutions are offered as to how television science programming might be improved and how media education can improve the quality of both viewing and understanding by enabling viewers to become critically autonomous.

Press and public

The actual responses of viewers must be somewhat disconcerting for television producers. Perhaps that is why many of them take more notice of their colleagues' views or of the gross BARB ratings, particularly when the viewers and their responses are so inaccessible. They must also find press reactions occasionally unnerving. One review of the *Led by the Nose* programme in a local newspaper was particularly brutal.

Last night on TV

WHAT a con-trick! TV bosses pulled a fast one over millions of viewers last night, *thanks to a smelly piece of cardboard.*

After all the pre-publicity about experimental *aromavision.* The Real World (ITV) was a big let-down. The show was all about our sense of smell, yet the sum total of the information imparted was that there are lots of different smells, and that some people can smell them better than others. Most of us have known that since nursery school.

But to tell us the obvious, The Real World had a studio audience scratching and sniffing the bits of cardboard, and I and millions of other viewers, were doing the same thing at home.

And what a waste of time it was. Most of the cardboard fragrances smelled the same, and even then it was hard to tell whether the odour was like burnt rice pudding, mushrooms or leather.

The cards added nothing to the programme, and neither did the American expert expensively flown in specially for the show. He merely showed he was an expert in waffle.

Despite all the emphasis of the programme being about smell. I was left wondering about an entirely visual question. Was presenter Sue Jay wearing that multi-hued shirt in order to win a bet? Or should the next Real World deal with the prevalance of colour-blindness?

Lucy Hughes-Hallet of *The Standard* also complained about the 'nervous mickey-taking' in the same programme.

The *Dead as the Dodo!* programme raised some doubts in one critic's mind about its approach.

S. Wales Evening Post
15/6/85

Such criticisms are usually balanced by more appreciative comments, such as this one on the 1986 series:

Yorkshire Evening Post
4/8/86

There is a recurrent concern, however, with the style of presentation:

Today 7/7/86

Sue Jay and Michael Rodd came up with more questions than answers I'm afraid, and there were so many ifs and buts that the whole subject bordered at times on science fiction which is not good for a programme entitled *The Real World*.

All in all the programme was probably one of the most entertaining I have seen for ages. Presenters Michael Rodd and Jackie Spreckley coped with the whole bizarre business with just the right touch of respectful cynicism. I loved it.

. . . at times, it was a little difficult to know whether one was in a lecture room or a music hall.

This kind of dissatisfaction was developed more fully in *The Listener* by John Naughton in a review of several science programmes. He contrasts a traditional view of science with an alternative one. He argues that *The Real World* 'is disposed to believe that scientific knowledge represents absolute truth' and contrasts this with the view that 'nothing can with certainty be known to be true'. He also found a programme he reviewed earlier 'jerky and unconvincing' but admitted that other viewers he had discussed it with had found it interesting, useful and informative. In other words, 'it probably worked'.

Audience research

The views of critics (and their friends) may be very public but they are by no means an accurate guide to how audiences actually respond. Nor does more extensive audience research using standardised viewing-group discussions produce more than occasionally illuminating impressions. Silverstone's study draws on the responses of eight groups of eight viewers consulted by the BBC's Broadcasting Research Department. His most significant finding is the extreme variety of viewers' responses. 'It is extraordinary to note how in the group conversation so much was constructed and had a life of its own with only a tiny thread holding it to the content of the film' (Silverstone, 1985, p. 192). He also expresses surprise in finding, as we have done in our research, how little factual content is remembered accurately.

It is important to realise, however, that any deliberate attempt to gauge responses automatically produces results which are different from normal audience reactions. This applies equally to the Audience Appreciation Index, on which *The Real World* consistently scores so well. Anyone who understands something about questionnaire methodology will realise that such information needs to be treated with great care.

The response of viewers is clearly dependent not only on the merits of individual programmes but also on a more general predisposition towards particular types of programme. Even the most generalised public image of particular television channels can work in favour of or against particular programmes even being watched. IBA research on a quota sample of 1,000 adults in 1985 showed that only 4% of respondents thought that ITV did the best job for science and Nature programmes, compared with 35% for BBC1. The same sort of perception applied to documentaries (ITV 11%: BBC1 34%) and to educational programmes (ITV 9%: BBC1 28%). A year later, the gap was much the same for each category (ITV 7%; 11%; 12%: BBC1 36%; 41%; 30%). The belief in BBC2's effectiveness for these kinds of programme is about the same as BBC1's. So there is clearly a very strong predisposition against ITV in this area.

There are other forms of predisposition. Although 60% of adult viewers appear to be interested in science and technology, there is disproportionate representation from older viewers, male viewers, those with more formal education and those from social classes A, B, or C1 according to a recent survey carried out by the BBC's Broad-casting Research Department. Young people appear to be less in-terested: in a small-scale survey carried out locally amongst a dozen tertiary college students, science documentary programmes were ranked next to bottom in a range of television programmes of different categories.

But such expressions of confidence in particular channels and levels of interest in science do not necessarily reflect actual viewing habits. The same BBC survey showed that 90% of respondents rated TV as their largest single source of information about science: yet one in five respondents did not actually watch any.

Predispositions are also evident in viewers' approaches to particu-lar programmes. Watching *Horizon* is not the prerogative of particu-lar social groups, but it is watched more selectively (i.e. on the basis of interest in a particular edition) than *Tomorrow's World.* It offers different kinds of pleasure and satisfaction; a challenge rather than reassurance. Yet nearly everyone (98%) who claims to watch *Horizon* also watches *Tomorrow's World.* This confirms that viewing preferences vary with context and occasion. Finally, it is not surprising to find that those viewers who are more confident in their understanding of science express doubts and disagreement about the content of science programmes. Conversely, viewers without such confidence tend not to express questions or doubts.

In the research carried out before and after the transmission of the 1986 series of *The Real World*, it was evident that only 34% of respondents claimed any awareness of the programme's existence, only 29% knew which channel it was on and only 16% claimed ever to have watched it. By comparison, over 96% were aware of *Horizon* and *Tomorrow's World*, and 78% and 91% respectively claimed to have watched them: 93% also knew that the latter is shown on BBC1. Given the short run of *The Real World*, the long gap between its annual appearances and the fact that it only ran for five years in comparison with over twenty for the BBC programmes, these differences are not surprising. But they do suggest audience problems for any ITV company producing a science programme. Although the number who claimed to have watched the series in 1986 only increased to 35% in this survey, it would have encouraged the TVS production team to know that awareness of the programme increased to 72%.

The average Audience Appreciation score for documentaries and features is about 79. *Tomorrow's World* generally reaches the high

70s and *The Real World* sometimes exceeds that. The *Dead as the Dodo?* programme achieved a score of 77. The BARB Audience Reaction Service also provides a more detailed qualitative breakdown of viewers' responses. The *Dead as the Dodo?* programme scored between 70% and 80% (amongst a sample of nearly 300 viewers) on such criteria as informativeness, interest and presentation. Over 80% felt that the subject-matter was well explained. Slightly fewer (75%) felt they had learned a great deal from it. It must also be encouraging to the production team that the programme appeared to be specifically chosen (rather than viewed through inertia) by nearly 70% of viewers and 76% felt they were likely to watch further programmes in the series.

But there is a problem with these impressive and reassuring figures. All the measures are entirely subjective estimates by the respondents themselves and no attempt is made to validate their accounts by any other criteria. It is also extraordinarily difficult to do badly on these measures. There is a notorious discrepancy between the numbers of people who tell market researchers that they wish to or do watch factual and informative programmes, and the numbers who actually switch on. Further, what they do when they have switched on is inaccessible to this kind of research. The question of what they in fact learn as a result is at one further remove. The feeling of having learned a great deal is very different from the fact of having done so. This may explain the apparent discrepancy between a high 'appreciation' of *The Real World*'s motivating features and the fact that the *Dodo* programme presents learning difficulties. It may be, as Silverstone and many other researchers have concluded, that broadcast television is simply not very effective in direct teaching. 'Broadcasting research suggests time and time again that viewers' ideas and opinions are rarely changed significantly by what they see in a single programme' (Silverstone, 1985, p. 182). An alternative explanation of this discrepancy would be that *The Real World* is good at creating an educative atmosphere but not at fulfilling a traditional educational function.

Programmes and viewers

Inevitably, in the interaction between programmes and viewers, the programme is the dominant element and is mainly responsible for the meanings generated. Even so, individual viewers bring to it their own interests, experience and culture. This personal baggage is unique to each viewer and will ultimately shape what he or she takes from the programme.

The *Dead as the Dodo?* programme urges the viewer to a particular view of science which derives from the 'common sense' one that scientific investigation is worthwhile, often exciting, and in the long run of great benefit to mankind. The thrust of the programme demands compliance. Are we given examples of scientific cul-de-sacs, or given space to reflect on the many ethical concerns which may be linked to 'progress'? Even so, will viewers necessarily comply with the argument of the programme? Will some take a view that asks questions which the programme sets out to avoid?

Perhaps the very diversity of viewers' responses is the reason why they are so hard to evaluate. Of course, programmes constrain the possible responses of viewers, just as the political and economic contexts of broadcasting constrain the programmes themselves. Yet any detailed work on a television programme reveals a clear variety and divergence of response from viewers. As Stanley Fish puts it, 'the reader's response is not to the meaning; it *is* the meaning' (Fish, 1980, p. 3).

The Real World clearly does not aim itself at school-age viewers. Usually, less than 10% of its audience is under 16. Yet this young audience is just about as large as *The Real World's* 35–44 year-old audience and appears to value the programme to almost the same extent as other age-groups. It is therefore an age-group which can provide as well as any other a basis for a different kind of analysis of viewer response from that which broadcasters normally use. Instead of examining the impact of the programme on viewers we can look at what viewers do with the programme.

Messages and meanings

Analysing programmes is, of course, much easier than studying responses, especially with the help of a video recorder. But content analysis has often provided a platform for dubious assumptions about a programme's effects on its audience. It has often been assumed that frequency of representation automatically produces an equivalent frequency of response in viewers. Although stereotypes are self-evident features of broadcast television, are they necessarily potent features of viewers' thinking and behaviour as a result?

Several studies of the technical codes used by television to present

speakers have emphasised how camera angle and framing indicate an attitude towards the speaking subject. Hence newsreaders, 'experts' and sometimes royalty are privileged in addressing the camera directly while most people are shown in two-thirds profile. However, it appears that the very codes which signal authority and respect to adults produce quite the opposite response in children. Those with a lot to *say* are quickly recognised and dismissed by children as less interesting (and so, less worthy of attention) than those who *act*.

Nevertheless, content analysis has yielded useful information. Studies of television have repeatedly shown overwhelming bias in the presentation of male and female gender roles. Content analyses have demonstrated that men figure in television programmes disproportionately to their actual representation in the population. Butler and Paisley concluded in a survey of 13 separate studies that the television ratio was roughly 7:3, whereas in most populations women outnumber men. A study by Dominick of 1,314 American television programmes from 1953 to 1977 found that shows exclusively starring women never constituted more than 14% of prime-time programmes, compared with an average of 45% for shows starring men in the same period. Other findings from a very large number of surveys show that men are more often seen in employment than women. Women, on the other hand, are very frequently represented as housewives; they are usually younger than men; their marital status is revealed more often than men's; and they are less likely to be seen in higher employment positions. Where women are presented with higher occupational status, it is likely to be linked with personal unhappiness or failure. Interaction between males and females on television reflects these different status positions. Perhaps the most striking characteristic is that men account for between 84% and 94% of 'voice-overs' in television advertisments. Since 'voice-overs' are almost invariably constructed as authoritative statements about the value of products or as trustworthy invitations to recommended courses of action, this dominance of the male voice is a powerful index of stereotyped gender representation on television.

Many of these findings are even more exaggerated in children's programmes. In a study of American educational programmes all the leading characters were male. In children's advertisements, the ratio of male to female was found to be 8:2. Finally, an analysis of children's advertisements revealed significant differences in their form according to the sex of the intended audience. Advertisements for boys showed more activity, were louder and more dramatic than the quieter advertisements for girls, which contained more soft background music and used fades and dissolves in the visual track far more frequently.

However, as Durkin points out, no amount of content analysis can establish whether any influence is exerted. It cannot tell us anything about the actual responses or about any longer-term consequences.

There seems to be a whole range of beliefs about television viewing which may derive from cultural snobbery, from the fact that television is viewed by large numbers of people simultaneously and from the fact that large sums of money are involved in the television industry. Does a Shakespeare play necessarily become mass entertainment if shown on television? Clearly, this will depend not only on the production values of the programme but also on the quality of attention brought to it by viewers. Is it possible to have a *non*-mass entertainment response to *Coronation Street*, given the right form of attention? Since it has become accepted to consider literature not as a series of fixed texts but as the label given to the objects of a certain kind of attention, could this kind of attention not also be given to television?

There are clearly formal and presentational differences between television and literature. These differences are crucial to explaining how and why attention is given or withheld. Both media rely on signs and codes which are apprehended visually (although television of course has an additional auditory channel). The clusters of words on the page or patterns of dots on the screen are the material forms which generate meaning. However, there is an essentially subjective imaging process which occurs in reading which is less necessary in television viewing. The fact that familiar forms constantly recur on television can also lead to a kind of visual fixation on what is comfortable rather than what is disturbing.

Some recent research has demonstrated the mismatch between the transmitted text and the received meaning of television programmes. Lewis, for example, in his article in Drummond and Patterson's *Television in Transition*, has shown how the input of viewers determines which units of meaning in a given programme will be understood and even *how* they will be understood. In other words, relevant pre-existent experience or knowledge is necessary to achieve the desired response. With news programmes, this becomes an acute problem. However 'meaningful' news happens to be, it still deals in narratives which are usually remote from viewers' experience. This is obviously even more so with children. For them, the potential meaning of some information is simply not communicated. If they do not have the necessary contextual knowledge, they cannot make sense of the narrative items. The result, at best, is a misreading, at worst, non-reading.

News presentation, according to Lewis, does very little to make narratives any easier to grasp. Compared with the continuous serial (which compels attention by involving viewers in the development of inter-linked story-lines) news fails signally. Its structure ensures that crucial information is given away early in 'headline' form at the beginning of each bulletin and of each item, and is then repeated for good measure at the end. The most important items are scheduled first and the whole bulletin (unlike a good story) gets less and less interesting the longer it goes on. At the same time, the overall flow of news bulletins is often erratic and demands constant readjustment of focus by viewers. All of these factors conspire to deny any form of pleasure which might arise for the viewer from participation in a developing narrative. It is perhaps no wonder that many adults and most children dislike the news and find it instantly forgettable, preferring instead close involvement with a good story.

In many ways, television apparently addresses its viewers as individuals, despite its function as a mass medium. But these individuals are categorised by television into viewers of soap-operas or serials, news, drama or documentaries. These categories of viewer are then identified with particular time-slots. In marketing terms, this enables broadcasters to 'position' their programmes to reach specific kinds of viewer. The sense of individuality created for viewers is merely a result of television's characteristically personalised mode of address – a mode which masks the generality of its assumptions. The same process occurs in the construction of the family as the viewing unit for television programmes. This is made explicit during public holidays, which are conceived by broadcasters as national family occasions. The mode of perception is individual but the context of viewing is the family in its normal domestic setting. Viewers are constructed in this way as 'normal citizens' who are part of a family unit, and as members of a specific nation with its own social and cultural practices. As Jean-Luc Godard puts it, 'Television doesn't make programmes – it makes viewers'.

Television's concern with audiences as quantities, however, can cause some misapprehensions. A statistical account of the number of viewers watching any particular episode of a serial disguises the fact that the actual membership of the audience may change from episode to episode. In the same way, the categorisation of audiences according to different kinds of programmes disguises the fact that television viewing may cross many of these supposed boundaries. Viewers use varied criteria for watching different kinds of programme, in particular according to social contexts. Hence, the way they approach programmes has an important bearing on the meanings which the programmes can achieve.

Audiences can be seen, on the one hand, as the product of television institutions and television programmes. On the other hand, audiences may be seen as specific groups within cultures or subcultures who are defined by particular social and economic relationships. These relationships are themselves the products of such social variables as class, race, gender, age and locality. They determine the particular 'meaning systems' and therefore actual understandings which audiences bring to programmes. If, in a general sense, programmes make audiences, in a very precise sense, audiences also make programmes. As Len Masterman puts it, 'Audiences work upon texts in complex and different ways, just as much as texts work upon audiences' (Masterman, 1985, p. 227). The audience has therefore a dual nature, as McQuail explains: 'It is a collectivity either formed in response to media content and defined by attention to that content, or one that exists already in social life and is then "catered for" by a particular media provision. Not infrequently, it is inextricably both at the same time' (McQuail, 1983, p. 149).

Understanding audiences' responses demands a movement away from individual psychology towards the subcultural groupings which define particular audiences and therefore the potential meanings of television programmes.

Mapping responses

A framework within which this can be done has been developed by Stuart Hall. He suggests that all 'readings' of cultural texts can be defined within three broad categories: the dominant, the negotiated and the oppositional. Viewers of a television programme are to be seen as producing a dominant or 'preferred' reading of a programme if they understand it largely as transmitted. If they read it in a different way by exploiting contradictions within it and subverting its overt meanings, they are producing an oppositional reading. If, on the other hand, producers and readers do not share the same codes and conventions so that the overt meanings are not comprehensible, then misreading or 'aberrant decoding' occurs. In practice, most readings are inevitably negotiated. To quote Stuart Hall:

> When the reader (viewer) takes the meaning full and straight, he is operating within the preferred interpretation of the message: that is, he is inside the *dominant* ideology. When the reader only imperfectly inhabits the code, and negotiates between the dominant and his own reading of the message, he is within the *negotiated* version of the dominant ideology. When the dominant code is refused, and a different code is brought in which 'detotalises' the preferred reading, the reader is within an *oppositional* ideological perspective. (Cohen & Young, 1981, p. 67)

These broad categories provide only a logical rather than a sociological framework for different readings of television. They do not equate in a simple, mechanical way with the different socio-economic positions of viewers. Nor do they establish a necessary correlation between demographic or sociological factors and specific responses.

David Morley has explored the nature and extent of the 'fit' between the socio-economic positions and the actual responses of young television viewers. After viewing recordings of two current affairs series on BBC1, groups with different backgrounds, ages, occupations and political allegiances were interviewed. The analysis of the interviews showed that responses to the programmes covered a very wide range of differences which were not directly correlated with social variables. Five groups of late adolescent students in Further Education, most of whom were female and black, were apparently so alienated from the programmes by the huge gap between their culture and what was represented that they could hardly make any sense at all of the items within the programmes.

These findings, along with those of Lewis, should be of some concern to broadcasters. For researchers they certainly provide a much more useful 'map' than any earlier work of how audience responses are both socially structured and relatively autonomous. At the same time they offer a powerful way of linking psychological perspectives on individual response with sociological perspectives on groups, institutions and ideology.

More recent work by Morley has taken this approach further by examining responses to television within a family context. We have used some of the methods he has evolved in our own study of responses to *The Real World*. By definition, most 'readings' will be the preferred or dominant ones for any given text. The data which the BARB survey produced suggest that this is also true for *The Real World*. Here, however, we can look at a selection of negotiated and oppositional readings in order to see what light they throw on how *Dead as the Dodo?* was understood by viewers.

First of all, we need to acknowledge that not all readings are equally valid. Some are the result of mistakes, errors and confusions and are better thought of as *mis*readings. Even so, they offer some insight into the way in which the understanding of a programme comes from an interaction between viewers and text.

Some of the misunderstandings shown by two different fourth-year classes were very basic:

Teacher	Can anybody tell me what cloning is?
All	(Silence)
Viewer 1	Cleaning something . . .
Teacher	Cleaning?
Viewer 1	You know, going through it . . .
Teacher	Where did you get that idea?
Viewer 1	They took the mummy apart and brushed it, didn't they . . . they did the same with the head . . . used a toothbrush for inside the head . . . cleaned the (?) then they said it about the magazine on the front.

The programme can hardly be blamed for this confusion of cloning with a wash-and-brush-up or for another viewer reading Baltic amber as traffic-lights. Similar misunderstandings occurred amongst adults in family viewing contexts:

Mother	They have given it a name, haven't they? That . . . thing . . . the protein and all that. It's the name they gave to a specific thing they were talking about. I thought he was saying 'DM'.

The father in the same family also had difficulty with the concept of DNA but was more pragmatic and generous in making allowances for the programme:

> Father   It's difficult. If you go into explaining everything it's going to make it a much longer programme and less interesting . . . Certainly I still don't know what DNA is.

This brings us back to the problem of the programme's rhythm and pace. It is a problem which occurs even in programmes which are specifically designed for educational uses, as is shown in recent research by Bentley and Watts for the IBA on science education programmes. One fourth-year girl they interviewed felt that she was actually missing much of the programme: 'half of what we watched must have gone out of our minds totally'. Another fourth-year girl in the same study offered an intelligent explanation of how this might happen:

> '. . . it went from one thing to another quite quickly, so that your mind's trying to catch up with what's happening. So maybe if they held the shot a bit longer when they finished speaking you could better see what's happening and try to understand what they've just said; and then go on to the next thing so you can understand all of it.'

Michael Svennevig's research on *Horizon* for the BBC's Broadcasting Research Department revealed very similar problems of keeping pace with rapid shifts of topic and location. Many details of the narrative were lost and the structure was often found to be too complex. Clearly, no viewer can be expected to grasp all of a programme's details, but it seems that some viewers have more problems than producers generally acknowledge.

Occasionally, we can see how misunderstandings may begin to form themselves into oppositional readings. It is as if the cracks in the programme are filled with the viewer's own material, as this comment from a family group suggests:

> Mother   I think it would be better if they kept the things we have got now, rather than bringing back the thingybobs. You've got to be a bit practical. You can't bring back everything.

Such a down-to-earth and homely perspective offers quite a challenge to producers. Sometimes, the original material supplied by the viewer may seem somewhat bizarre, or at least very distant from the focus of the text. Nowhere does *Dead as the Dodo?* mention the humble hamster, but the following exchange shows very clearly how one fourth-year student brought his own personal concerns to bear on the programme's argument:

Viewer 1	. . . it's the same as make-up . . . it's not needed . . . like only the scientists want to know if they can do it, that's all.
Viewer 2	If an animal's gone then you should let it be gone . . . you're not going to get anything out of it, are you?
Viewer 3	I'd like to see a dinosaur about!
Viewer 1	They'd never do that anyway.
Viewer 3	Yes they would, he said so.
Viewer 1	I breed hamsters and there is one group that is totally extinct, well not quite totally and that's the dark grey . . . and . . . if you bring two hamsters together and say you get a light grey . . . and you breed this light grey with a darker colour and it comes out to a dark grey, if you keep on, er . . . interbreeding these grey then you eventually come out with a proper dark grey . . . then you bring it back, so it's pretty easy isn't it?
Teacher	So you're saying rather than go to cloning go to cross-breeding?
Viewer 1	Yeh. So if you cross a horse and a zebra you get a zagga.
Teacher	Quagga.

This kind of alternative reading represents for some viewers an ethical position, especially for more experienced and confident ones. One second-year A-level student who watched the programme commented:

'Why play havoc with them? They know what they need to know about the dodo . . . it's raping history as well, isn't it . . .? Really you're playing with other people's lives . . . You're playing God.'

Others in this group went further and offered their own critique of the programme's style:

'I think the level of programme presentation was us as being morons'.

'A bit patronising, the presenters ... and when they had that monkey thing ... the idea of using it was bad actually. I mean it reduced your intelligence to nothing ... if we were younger we wouldn't find it patronising. If we were older we would turn it off'.

One of them was even able to offer a comment on what he saw as the programme's ideology: 'It made it look a bit rosy ... there should be a bit more sort of honesty ... it's selling "science is right".'

Whatever the individual responses of these viewers, their wide-ranging discussion of the programme made it very clear that they brought their own ideas and their own agenda to the programme. It was with these predispositions that the programme had to communicate.

Conceptual map of small-group discussion amongst adolescent viewers

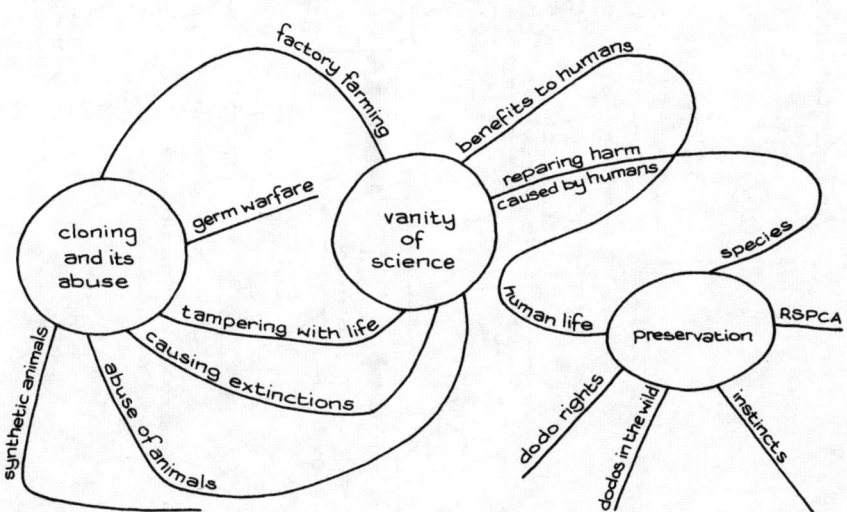

An individual map of *Dead as the Dodo?*

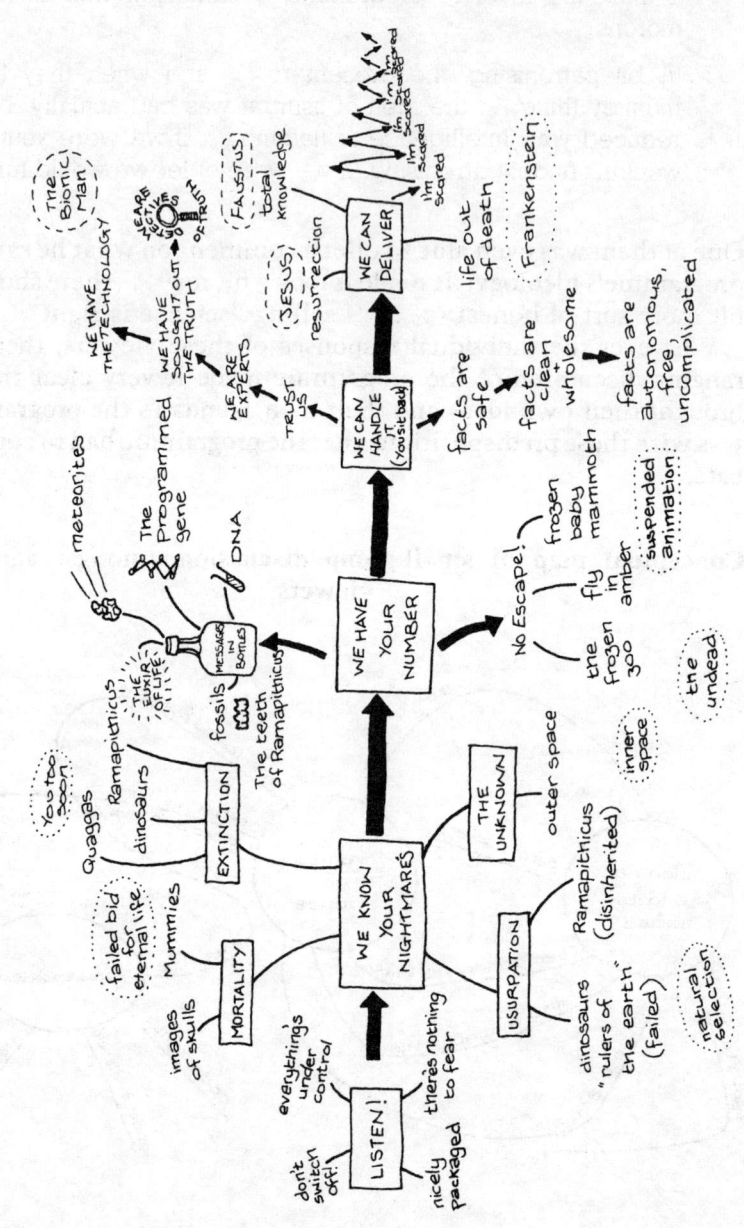

Creating a dialogue

As well as offering certain forms of pleasure, it is the acknowledged task of programmes like *The Real World* to enhance our understanding of the significance of science. At the very least, they undertake to reduce misunderstanding and not introduce more confusion. In order to do this, they need to make connections within individual programmes. They also need to make connections with individual viewers' experience, so that viewers can bring to bear the relevant knowledge and understanding which will enable them to respond critically and constructively to the issues raised.

Wolfgang Iser has written, 'Whenever the flow . . . is interrupted, the opportunity is given to us to bring into play our own faculty for establishing connections' (Iser, 1974, p. 280). The main problem with *Dead as the Dodo?* seems to be that it rarely pauses for breath. It does not provide gaps for viewers to slide into in order to develop their understanding. The ceaseless flow of the narrative closes off too many issues without examining or explaining them and, as a result, many viewers switch into a mode of attention which does not help clarify the programme's argument. The gaps that do exist, as has already been suggested, are in the argument's logic and are not ones which invite a dialogue with viewers. The danger of this is noted by Michael Svennevig in his comments on responses to *Horizon*:

> For many individuals, *A New Green Revolution?* left more questions unanswered than answered, in that 'obvious' questions were not asked – such as *how* peasant farmers could lose their lands in the first place, or *why* irrigation schemes failed. The result was that they then supplied what they believed to be equally valid but different answers and conclusions to those offered in the programme. With these 'gaps' seen in the argument, they could not then fully accept the points made, and alternatives, prejudices and preconceptions remained unchallenged.   (Svennevig, 1984, p. 4)

How can this danger be avoided? Gardner and Young suggest an ambitious set of goals for television science programming which might enable dialogue and debate to increase:

– To move from science as cultural consumption to science as critique.

- To move from the content of science as progress to an analysis of the constitution of science, technology and medicine, of their labour processes and of their articulations with other practices.
- To move from the 'impact' of science to the process of constitution of its research programme, opening up to public scrutiny and prioritisation the origination of issues, facts and artifacts.

A humbler (but longer) set of goals is offered for educational science programmes by Bentley and Watts. Amongst thirteen recommendations, these stand out as most relevant to *The Real World*:

- contextualisation of issues
- positive images of women and other cultures in relation to science
- clear and explicit structures
- challenge to popular preconceptions
- personal, social and technological relevance
- science as a human and social construction

It is sometimes assumed that programmes' styles are limited by their audiences' capacities. But this is only partially true. The development of new forms of programming and even, as with Channel 4, the growth of new channels, suggests that innovation is possible. Assumed audience responses do place some constraints on what is possible at a given moment. But programme makers' assumptions about responses are sometimes wrong and viewers' reactions are often unpredictable. As we have shown, there are also other more powerful and more complex structural and professional factors at work.

It is very likely that audience reactions to television programmes are partially conditioned by what is provided (as the growth in awareness of *The Real World* over its 1986 run suggested). The provision of different kinds of programme might well meet audience needs which are not yet known. Factual programmes can attract large audiences and they can attract thoughtful audiences. As Michael Svennevig explains: 'For some people 'science' is an unknown area of knowledge, which can be impenetrable and off-putting. For others, scientific principles are part of everyday life, and 'science' is not a label for the unknown' (Svennevig, 1984, p. 1).

But the responsibility is not entirely that of the programme producers. We also have responsibilities as viewers. Responses to science programmes are closely related to educational experience, as are responses to television itself. Education about media therefore has a particularly significant role to play.

Critical autonomy

Valuing the real world of viewers' experience and imagination is an important feature of media education. It aims for more than the metaphors of 'reading' and 'tele-literacy' imply. Developing a habit of critical reflection towards television entails realising that programmes are constrained by their viewers as well as by their producers.

The language of television is one which we all share – as producers, parents, viewers and participants. Any development of its educative and informative power can only come from developing this common language. Producers can clearly learn a great deal from viewers. At the same time, viewers can usefully learn much more about television. In the long run, learning about television can take us beyond the basic function of understanding the medium towards a wider and deeper understanding of the 'real world' which television represents and which we all inhabit.

APPENDIX A

Programme Transcript

MICHAEL RODD   This man is having his head examined. Not that it'll bother him. He's dead, and has been for . . . eight thousand years. What is amazing is that there is anything inside his skull at all.

This is the oldest human brain ever to be investigated – and it's offering us vital clues in an extraordinary scientific detective story that will perhaps one day answer the biggest question of all – where did we come from?

SUE JAY   Who or even what were our earliest ancestors?

Did we all emerge from primeval sludge? Or is there the fantastic possibility that we came from somewhere else wafted here on a particle of meteoric dust?

MICHAEL RODD   And in the course of trying to find out where we came from, could there be a possibility that forms of life we once thought dead and gone for ever could walk the earth again. Have we really seen the last of the dodo?

This recent headline from an American newspaper, famous for its exaggeration, may be a little too imaginative – but surely the same can't be said about this one, from one of the world's most important scientific journals. DNA, the chemical foundation of life itself, cloned from a two thousand year-old Egyptian mummy.

SUE JAY   Tonight we're going to try to unravel the mystery
           of our past. To help us to do it — this
           unprepossessing chap. Actually he's a bit of a
           mystery himself . . . at this end he's clearly
           horse . . .

MICHAEL RODD   Whilst at this, he is obviously more like a zebra.

           He is, or rather was, because he's been extinct a
           hundred years, a quagga, surely one of the
           unluckiest of all animals. Hunted into oblivion
           on the plains of South Africa, only months before a
           law made him a preserved species. But he's
           achieved distinction in extinction because he
           plays an historic part in our search for the past.

SUE JAY   How life on this planet evolved to produce man has
           always fascinated us — but not so long ago all we
           had to go on was just bones. And there is a limit to
           what a dry bone can tell anyone.

           But surprise, surprise, over the last few years,
           scientists have realised that these dried-up
           remains still contain tiny amounts of protein.
           What are proteins?

           Well, they're the material that once filled these
           channels in the bone when the creature was still
           alive. Proteins are a vital ingredient not only of
           bones, but of the fleshier parts of the body — the
           parts which have long since disappeared. Finding
           out that proteins can still linger was a big
           breakthrough.

MICHAEL RODD   Within the last six months it's been demonstrated
           in California that it's possible to extract even
           the original instructions from which these
           proteins were made, the very foundation of life
           itself — DNA — and that is going to tell us a great
           deal about where we came from.

           This is human DNA. In this sticky viscous chemical
           are all the instructions which make up an
           individual from the colour of the eyes to the size
           of the feet. Now most of us assume that when we die

158 Appendix A

this dies with us. So the first step in tonight's story was taken when scientists questioned that assumption.

We pick up the next link in our detective story here in the zoo here in San Diego in California, where the animals are playing a part in helping to determine how life is as it is and where it goes from here. Quite painlessly under anaesthetic, as part of other routine investigations, small nicks are taken from many of the animals' ears and these skin and blood vessel samples are then stored in a very different sort of zoo – a modern Noah's Ark in which as many of the world's creatures as possible will be represented.

Geneticist, Doctor Oliver Ryder

DR RYDER The frozen zoo was established to make the dwindling genetic resources of animals like endangered species available for future scientists to study. In some cases we may not be able to prevent the extinction of species, but the essential genetic foundations – the germ nucleus of these species – can be preserved, but it's equally clear to us that we have no comprehension of some of the future uses to which these genetic resources might usefully be put.

MICHAEL RODD But in 1982 Ryder received a sample he felt even he couldn't handle. This animal was extinct. There are a few photographs of one taken a century ago, in London Zoo, but exterminated in its native South Africa in the 1860s, the very last quagga mare died alone, in the zoo in Amsterdam in 1883. Everyone thought that was that.

But in 1979, whilst renovating a complete family of the animals which had been stuffed originally 150 years ago, a quagga expert in South Africa had realised that the original job of preservation had, in this case, not been done very thoroughly.

DR RYDER   Reinhold Rau of the South African Museum sent me
            the quagga material and he wondered whether the
            tissue would be worthwhile. But it was very
            clear when I got it that it would be very useful
            because one can see veins in it, one could see if
            you looked under the microscope that there was
            the dried blood of the quagga in these veins. And
            so I was optimistic it would be possible to gain
            information from the protein still in these
            samples about the question of what was the
            quagga.

MICHAEL RODD   A final answer to that was to be found in a
            laboratory across the bay from San Francisco in
            Berkeley. This is where Ollie Ryder sent some of
            his precious quagga samples, inspired by the
            work being done here in the department of
            biochemistry. Here Doctor Russell Higuchi
            believed he could extract from the fragments of
            the extinct half-horse, half-zebra, the most
            fundamental genetic finger-print of all – DNA –
            the complex instructions from which all the
            different proteins that made up the living
            quagga were initially created. But if he could
            extract it, would it be in fit shape to be cloned,
            to be copied in the lab, over and over again for
            research and investigation?

            He identified a solvent to strip out any DNA,
            introduced a virus to link up with any DNA and
            added bacteria . . . with which the virus, now
            carrying any quagga DNA, would react. Culture
            plates like this one revealed minute quantities
            of DNA were present – perhaps only about a
            millionth of the total picture when the quagga
            was alive, but enough to be cloned and enough to
            reveal a strong similarity to today's zebras and
            horses.

            In this case, a dot in the lower column indicates
            a match with a zebra. The comparatively few
            letters show where the DNA of today's zebra does
            not correspond with that of its extinct close
            relative.

Higuchi had succeeded in extracting tiny but very valuable fragments of the chemical foundation of a life-form that ceased to exist a hundred years ago.

DR HIGUCHI   The kind of information we want can still be found in these very small fragments and within these fragments the sequence of preservation was very good and accurate to a point where we don't think there is very much change at all — even though it's been dead for a hundred years.

MICHAEL RODD   For Higuchi and his colleagues this was just reward after the considerably less successful work on the tissue samples from Deema, a baby mammoth, found almost perfectly preserved after some ten thousand years in the permanent ice of Siberia. Up to now the mammoth had resisted all attempts at DNA extraction, but the success with the quagga makes it well worthwhile working to increase the sensitivity of Higuchi's now proven techniques. Because it's clear that minute fragments of DNA, not just from the mammoth, but from creatures like the dinosaur, even longer extinct, might just be identifiable.

DR RYDER   Russell's work is very significant, the quagga is but a single animal — however noteworthy. The greater impact is that we are now using the technology that he has developed so well and have the opportunity to go back and learn about the genetic structure of long gone animals.

Whereas heretofore we could only base our analysis on what their appearance basically was now we can actually, theoretically at least, if we can find some dried tissue, just a bit here and there, we can go back and find out what its genes were like.

SUE JAY   The thing to remember in all this is the widely held belief that all life came from one original source and evolved in a variety of ways. So, as scientists work their way backwards in time through the mammoth, even the dinosaurs themselves, we are getting closer to the original source of all life, including us.

MICHAEL RODD   Man's family tree stretches back through time with our line branching away from those of our closest living relatives – the chimps, the gorillas, the orangutans and so on over millions of years. But exactly when the breaks took place has always been a subject of great argument – an argument we can now settle. Meet the next clue in our detective story.

This is Ramapithecus. Now he goes back fourteen million years, and once upon a time we thought he was a man. More recently we have not been so sure. We have always known about the fourteen million years, though, from his teeth which were discovered. And when this was all the evidence we had we thought Rama was more closely related to us than he was to any of the apes. And because we were absolutely certain about the fourteen million years the evidence from this meant that our family tree had to look like this . . . And there he is, Ramapithecus, fair and square on our direct line. Clearly the earliest of men.

SUE JAY   But today there is new evidence to hand. Not only have we discovered more bones and teeth, but scientists have started to study the proteins and more recently the DNA of living animals including both apes and humans. And all of this indicates we're much nearer the apes than we thought.

MICHAEL RODD   In fact, if that new evidence is correct, all this is going to have to be re-drawn. Now it looks as though we humans broke away from the orangutans at ten, and from the gorillas and chimps a mere four million years ago. Why, this chap and I were as good as brothers.

SUE JAY   And all that put Ramapithecus in a rather embarrassing position. How can he go on

pretending that he is a man when all the evidence
suggests that he is, well, just another ape?
Ramapithecus faced an identity crisis and took
it to San Francisco where he found a doctor who
could solve his problem.

MICHAEL RODD   Dr Jerold Lowenstein regularly analyses
proteins from his hospital patients. In his
research work he's used the same standard
technique to examine protein extracted from the
teeth of Ramapithecus. If he could successfully
compare the proteins of today's apes and humans
with those of Ramapithecus, extinct for 15
million years, he believed he could help settle
whose ancestor Ramapithecus is.

JEROLD   Ramapithecus proteins were no more like human
LOWENSTEIN   proteins than they were like orangutan
proteins or chimpanzee proteins or gorilla
proteins. Therefore, my work strongly suggested
what the earlier molecular work had also
suggested, that Ramapithecus was an ape and not
a man.

MICHAEL RODD   But I think your work was fundamental in
achieving accord on this point, perhaps for the
first time ever?

JEROLD   Yes, I believe that it was critical but at the
LOWENSTEIN   same time people were finding other parts of
Ramapithecus besides the teeth and those other
parts also strongly suggested that it was not
human but an ape. So the new molecular data and
the new fossil data happened to go right along
with each other.

SUE JAY   So poor old Ramapithecus isn't really one of us
after all.

So what if we could examine not just the protein
of long-extinct creatures, but the chemical
instructions from which these proteins were made
— the DNA itself? The work on the quagga —
extinct for a hundred years — has proved that DNA

survives long after death. The question is, how long?

MICHAEL RODD   The Egyptian obsession with preserving their well-to-do citizens as mummies has long fascinated those investigating our past. But a team from Upsala in Sweden has just stolen all the scientific headlines by succeeding in cloning DNA from a mummy. Now such remains are at least two thousand years old. So DNA can survive a long time. But it takes persistence to find it. The Swedes tried no fewer than twenty-three mummies before they found any hint of clonable DNA. But even that achievement will be eclipsed by the next clue in our detective story.

Last year a team from the University of Florida, in Gainesville, who'd been working for two years on a site near the Kennedy Space Center at Cape Canaveral, made what is almost certainly the archaeological discovery of the decade – a skull of a human female, which initial tests suggested was of the order of seven thousand years old. The following day the skull of a 27-year-old male was unearthed. But it was only when these two vintage discoveries had been safely transported to the lab that the real significance of the finds became clear. During the standard wash and brush up to which all specimens like these are subjected, it appeared that there was more here than just bone and teeth. A routine hospital test followed and it revealed that inside the skull, there was something which looked like a brain. The back of one of the skulls was removed and a silence fell over the lab, as the team realised that it was looking at a human brain that had to be at least seven thousand years old. The quality of the discovery was later confirmed in tests with scanning machines and X-ray units. Through sheer luck the deep, peaty conditions of the Florida swamp had preserved the tissue of the brain over the years, though one had shrunk to a third of its life size and the other was about 60% of the size one would expect. What

mattered was that within the fragments of soft
tissue, there might just be human DNA, much
older than anything ever worked on before: DNA
which could be extracted.

In the lab the Gainesville team set to work on
what are almost certainly the oldest preserved
human brains in the world. The DNA strands from
the two brains now certified as around 8,000
years old, are readily identifiable. They are
clearly human. They are remarkably intact. But
the supply of material like this for research is
obviously limited. For the important detailed
detective work that now can be done on our
distant ancestors, this evidence has to be
cloned, to be copied, over and over again.

SUE JAY   Doctor Phil Laipis is one of the Gainesville
team and he's flown over to join us on The Real
World. Phil, can I ask you to describe that
moment when you realised what you've got is not
just a lump of earth clogging up the skull, but a
real brain?

DR LAIPIS There was just dead silence in the lab. I was
holding what was recognisably a human brain,
everyone had seen one and we knew what we had was
an eight thousand year-old brain. It was total
amazement; we had not expected that at all.

SUE JAY   What have you actually done with the brain since
that moment, what have you discovered about it?

DR LAIPIS There is a surprising amount of structure left
in the brain. There are some cells still intact.
We have been able to isolate DNA from that brain
— we have shown that at least some of the DNA is
human DNA. And we have been able to clone some
small fragments of DNA from the brain.

SUE JAY   What is the next step?

DR LAIPIS What we have to do is look at the DNA fragments we

have; we have to get more of them and match them
to known pieces of human DNA.

It's as if we had a sentence out of Hamlet, we
didn't know where it belonged and we were trying
to match it to the whole volume of Shakespeare.
We have those individual lines, we are trying to
match them now, to look for the 'To be or not to
be' soliloquy in Hamlet.

SUE JAY   But what's its real relevance, what are we going
to learn from all of this?

DR LAIPIS   We're going to learn (or the archaeologists in
particular are going to learn) where these
people came from. They may be able to learn
whether these people left any descendants. From
my point of view, we're going to learn about how
DNA survives — in the environment after the
individual is dead; how much damage occurs; how
much it has changed both from damage and just
from the normal evolutionary processes that have
happened over 8,000 years.

SUE JAY   Do you think that one day you may actually be
able to find out things about samples of DNA that
are even older?

DR LAIPIS   I think so. We know how much damage has occurred
here. I think that we will be able to go back
another perhaps 30,000 years, perhaps a little
bit longer, and if the DNA is as well preserved
we'll be able to clone that DNA as well — and that
will be much more interesting to me.

SUE JAY   It sounds it . . . . thank you very much indeed.

MICHAEL RODD   Should really elderly DNA prove viable, then
that would bring to a positive conclusion
perhaps the most intriguing element of all of
this story. It concerns a fruit-fly happily
buzzing through the sunshine that decided to
take a rest on the bark of a passing tree. It
wasn't a very good idea, because that particular

part of the tree was covered with gluey, oozy resin and the fly stuck fast. All this happened 23 million years ago in what is today the Dominican Republic. But over the years the resin hardened into amber, encasing the fly in a perfectly preserved time-capsule.

Today entomologist George Poinar working at Berkeley, believes that the evidence contained in this earliest of known preserved life-forms could, thanks to the techniques now perfected, prove extremely exciting.

GEORGE POINAR   The specimens that we have found in amber are interesting for two reasons. First of all they tell us what existed on Earth 20–40 million years ago, so we can have an idea of what kind of insects occurred here and how they compared with present-day forms to give us some idea of the evolution. Then they are interesting from the cellular stand-point because possibly we can revive some of the cells because we do find them in remarkable condition. In other words, we could possibly find DNA still inside the nucleii of some of these flies, preserved in Baltic amber which is 40 to 60 million years old.

MICHAEL RODD   Are you confident that the DNA in that amber is viable?

GEORGE POINAR   Well, if we found that it was viable this would open up a new chapter because no one really believes that DNA can be viable for such a long period. So we wouldn't confirm anything that we already knew. We would be opening a new area and providing some new evidence as to the longevity of nucleic acids and possibly, even in a broader scope, the origin of certain forms of life here on Earth. Because the DNA could remain viable for up to 40 million years, there's an indication that this is a time-period in which material could come from other planets, from other extra terrestrial sources and be brought here to planet Earth.

SUE JAY   What George Poinar is saying is that if the
            fruit-flies prove that DNA can survive 60 million
            years that would be long enough for some
            primitive life-form to make an exceedingly long
            journey arriving on earth on board one of these:
            a meteorite from space. If all life came from one
            original source, that is a real eye-opener.

MICHAEL RODD   Mind you, it's not a new suggestion. One eminent
            British scientist, Professor Fred Hoyle, has
            been claiming for years that life came from
            space. Who knows? Perhaps Sir Fred is right and a
            fruit-fly could confirm a link with the past which
            we all share somewhere beyond the stars.

SUE JAY   And from one idea which up to now has been
            regarded by most as a complete flight of fantasy,
            how about the equally incredible possibility
            that if we can extract DNA from quaggas,
            mammoths, even dinosaurs, perhaps one day we
            might reconnect these complex chemical chains so
            that creatures we once thought extinct could
            once again walk the earth?

            Can we any longer say with certainty that that
            will never happen?

DR LAIPIS   I wouldn't say never, we might get lucky, we
            might find the sample that has been perfectly
            preserved and we could have woolly mammoths
            going through Rocky Mountain National Park
            again. I'd like to try it.

DR RYDER   I can't foresee how this could come about in the
            future, but scientists are notoriously poor
            predictors of what the future will hold.

JEROLD   I think it's entirely possible but obviously we
LOWENSTEIN can't do it unless we have the program for a
            quagga or a mammoth, which consists of the total
            amount of DNA for these creatures. And so I think
            it behoves us to store that information and
            being able to clone them is just the technical
            problem. It may take another 20 or 30 or even a

hundred years, but I think eventually we will be able to do it.

MICHAEL RODD   Now if any of you find all this a little complicated, well it is, but just remember what it boils down to is this: the next time you find yourself face to face with a dodo, remember we did warn you — here on The Real World . . . Goodnight!

APPENDIX B

Responses from *The Real World* Team

Peter Williams (Controller of Factual Programmes)

I have two major concerns over *Making 'The Real World'*. The first is tactical. The often bantering exchanges that took place between the various members of the team are extracted, recorded and solemnly dissected, being given a conclusive *gravitas* that they do not warrant except as an illustration of the process by which decisions are made.

The second is strategic. It concerns the authors' understandable determination to draw general conclusions from specific limited experience. Scientists are, of course, wary about doing this.

Television has an honourable track record of questioning closely scientists and their work. John Willis' unit, in Yorkshire, has pursued the nuclear industry doggedly and with imagination. Here at TVS, we revealed the work of Patrick Steptoe and Robert Edwards on *in vitro* fertilisation, graphically explained the process by which they were trying to cure infertility, and raised most of the issues subsequently considered by the Warnock Committee. We did the same in Dayton, Ohio with Petrofsky's engineering solutions to spinal injuries; and in revealing the names of the Japanese scientists responsible for Japan's germ warfare experiments during World War II – in Unit 731.

The coverage of science on television isn't all that different from any other subject. You still need knowledge, flair and accuracy. Increasingly you need access – to places and to figures and to conclusions. By no means do I believe that makers of science programmes try to soothe away our anxiety about those men in white coats; certainly that is not part of the brief of *The Real World*.

Neither Greg Dyke nor I have spared any effort to persuade the network controllers to take the programme and give it a slot that will ensure it maximum exposure. It is an important strand in TVS' output and has been ever since we became the franchise holders. Our position as supplicant at the major controllers' table has meant, continually, that we have been unable to make long-term plans for the series.

Garfield Kennedy (Producer)

In *Dead as the Dodo*? it was my intention to make a production which let the audience see a glint of the sharp edge of one particular area of scientific endeavour. I could have chosen less demanding subject matter but I like to challenge the audience. It is better to try to place such science in a popular (prime-time) short (30 minute) slot than admit defeat and say, 'it's too difficult for a general audience'. You lose something of course. The short running time permits a taste rather than a meaty bite of the details of the complete story. In fact, to completely understand the science would require a couple of advanced science qualifications.

As producer of the programme I was aware of many of the moral implications of the subject matter. In fact they were precisely what drew me to the story in the first place. However, in the context of our programme, which acted as a first introduction for many to a complex area of modern science, there was no place to rigorously set up the political and moral debate. To have attempted this would have driven the programme away from this transmission slot and its mass audience, if for no other reason than the running time would have had to be longer. Therefore I welcome, but do not find surprising, [the] identification of moral questions arising from the programme. However, I am sure most viewers could see many of these implications too – it's what makes the programme relevant to us as lay men and women. I do not believe it was necessary to spoon-feed these thoughts to our audience. I am sure the programme opened doors in many people's minds, priming them to take further interest in the subjects covered and touched on. At the very least they were given a chance to know that this scientific work is going on.

This brings me to the issue of the 'completeness' of our programmes in the context of the whole series. While a formally structured educational course will correctly attempt to relate elements in one unit of study to the rest of the course, *The Real World* is a series of (broadly speaking) unrelated case studies. Contradictions in opinion and emphasis may occur when two *Real Worlds* are directly compared. There is no intention to apply an editorial three-line whip on the series as a whole. Rather the exposition of the diversity of scientific thought is a strong strand within the series ... We know we have a large but changing audience (in common with other series in the same transmission slot). Cross-referencing programme to programme would thus be a pointless exercise which would only irritate and confuse.

At the outset of our programme planning, we aim to look for the best science stories. With a series aimed primarily at a network UK audience we serve as an information source of what is happening in British science, and that which has relevance for a UK audience from overseas sources. There is no sense of jingoism in the planning of programmes. Rather the economics of television programme budgeting demand that we look close to home first. Luckily, and perhaps remarkably, we still find world-class science and scientists here on our doorstep.

Bibliography

Anghelides, P. 'Overrated ratings', *The Listener* (22 Jan. 1987)

Baggaley, J. *The Psychology of the Television Image* (Gower/Saxon House, 1980)
Bennett, T. *et al.* (eds.). *Popular Television and Film* (BFI/Open University, 1981)
Bentley, D. and Watts, M. *Looking for Learning* (IBA, 1986)
Bolton, R. 'Divided We Stand', *Broadcast* (22 Aug. 1986) 'The Centre Takes All', *Edinburgh International Television Festival Programme* (Aug. 1986)

Clare, A. 'The Courage to be Boring', *The Listener* (26 Jun. 1986)
Clarke, M. *Teaching Popular Television* (Heinemann/BFI, 1987)
Cohen, S. and Young, J. (eds.). *The Manufacture of News* (Sage Constable, rev.ed. 1981)
Coren, A. 'Nice Crackpots in the Clay Pit', *The Mail on Sunday* (8 Feb. 1987)

Department of Education and Science. *Popular Television and Schoolchildren: the Report of a Group of Teachers* (DES, 1983)
Dixon, B. 'The didactic element is too often missing', *The Listener* (23 Oct. 1980)
Drummond, P. and Patterson, R. *Television in Transition* (BFI, 1986)
Dunkley, C. *Television Today and Tomorrow* (Penguin, 1985)
Dunn, R. 'Science, Technology and Bureaucratic Domination: Technology and the Ideology of Scientism', *Media, Culture and Society* (1979)
Durkin, K. *Television, Sex Roles and Children* (Open University Press, 1985)

Eco, U. 'Can Television Teach?', *Screen Education*, 31 (Summer 1979)
Ellis, J. *Visible Fictions* (RKP, 1982)
Elstein, D. 'Why ITV's "Carve-up" is not "Fundamentally archaic"', *The Listener* (11 Jun. 1987)

Fish, S. *Is There a Text in This Class?* (Harvard University Press, 1980)
Forbes, P. 'Just Cash the Cheques and Get Away with the Minimum', *New Statesman* (29 May 1987)

Garnham, N. *Structures of Television* (BFI, 1980)
Goodhart, G. J. *et al. The Television Audience* (Saxon House 1975)

Hart, A. P. 'Finding the Intended Receiver', *The Listener* (30 April 1987)
Heath, S. and Skirrow, G. 'Television: A World in Action', *Screen, 18/2* (1977)

Independent Broadcasting Authority. *Annual Report and Accounts 1976–7* (IBA, 1977)
  Annual Report and Accounts 1985–6 (IBA, 1986)
  Attitudes to Broadcasting in 1985 (IBA, 1986)
  Attitudes to Broadcasting in 1986 (IBA, 1987)
  Television and Radio 1977 (IBA, 1977)
  Television and Radio 1987 (IBA, 1987)
  Television Programme Guidelines (IBA, 1985)
Iser, W. *The Implied Reader* (Johns Hopkins University Press, 1974)

James, C. *Glued to the Box* (Picador, 1983)
Jones, D. (ed.). *Open the Box* (Channel 4 pamphlet, 1986)

Lawson, H. 'The Fallacy of Scientific Objectivity', *The Listener* (20 Feb. 1986)
Lusted, D. and Drummond, P. (eds.). *Television and Schooling* (BFI, 1985)

Masterman, L. *Teaching the Media* (Comedia, 1985)
  (ed.) *Television Mythologies* (Comedia/MK Press, 1984)
Magee, B. *Popper* (Fontana, rev.ed. 1982)
McQuail, D. *Mass Communication Theory* (Sage, 1983)
Morley, D. *Family Television: Cultural Power and Domestic Leisure* (Comedia, 1986)
  The Nationwide *Audience* (BFI, 1980)

Naughton, J. 'Tee Cosy', *The Listener* (24 July 1986)
  'Dense Matter', *The Listener* (21 Aug. 1986)
Nisbett, A. 'Science on Television', *British Universities Film and Video Council News Letter* (Feb. 1984)

Popper, K. *Conjectures and Refutations* (Routledge, 4th ed. 1972)

Report of the Committee on Financing the BBC (HMSO, 1986)
Root, J. *Open the Box* (Comedia, 1986).
Royal Society. *Science Education 11–18 in England and Wales* (Royal Society, 1982)
Ryder, N. *Science, Television and the Adolescent* (IBA, 1982)

Sabbagh, K. 'Science as Entertainment', *See 4, 14* (1987)
Silverstone, R. *Framing Science: The Making of a BBC Documentary* (BFI, 1985)
Svennevig, M. *Research for* Horizon: A New Green Revolution? (BBC Broadcasting Research Dept, 1984)

Television South plc. *Report and Accounts 1985* (TVS, 1986)
  Report and Accounts 1986 (TVS, 1987)
  Report and Accounts 1987 (TVS, 1987)